Simple Pleasures
of the
GARDEN

Julia Bayne

February 18th 2017 Happy Birthday

To my beautiful daughter
Love
Mom
3/4/17

Simple Pleasures
of the
GARDEN

Stories, Recipes & Crafts *from the*
Abundant Earth

Susannah Seton

CONARI PRESS
Berkeley, California

First published in 1998 by Conari Press, a division of
Red Wheel/Weiser
368 Congress Street
Boston, MA 02210

Cover photography: Theresa Vargo
Cover art direction: Ame Beanland
Designed & electronically produced: Suzanne Albertson
Diagram illustrations: Joan Carol

Library of Congress Cataloging-in-Publication Data
Seton, Susannah, 1952–
Simple pleasures of the garden : stories, recipes & crafts
from the abundant earth / Susannah Seton.
p.   cm.
Includes index.
ISBN 1-57324-104-0 (hardcover)
ISBN 1-57324-501-1 (paperback)
1. Gardening.   2. Gardens.   3. Nature craft.
4. Cookery (Vegetables).   5. Seton, Susannah, 1952–   . I. Title.
SB455.S43   1998
635—dc21   97-46743

Printed in Canada
07 06 05 04   TCP   3 4 5 6 7 8 9 10

If you want to be happy
for an hour, have a party.
If you want to be happy for
a week, kill your pig and eat it.
But if you want to be happy
all your life, become
a gardener.

—Chinese Saying

Simple Pleasures of the Garden

Earthly Delights ix

*E*ARTHLY DELIGHTS

*The lesson I have thoroughly learnt, and wish
to pass on to others, is to know the enduring
happiness that the love of a garden gives.*

—Gertrude Jekyll

*L*ike many folks, pleasure is not a concept that is native to me. A serious, A student, high-achieving, puritanical type all my life, I've been what author Stella Resnick calls, in her book *The Pleasure Zone,* "pleasure resistant." It is only recently, in my mid-forties, that I have begun to try to focus on, indeed relish, the good things in life. The first step was to identify the things that gave me pleasure. In so doing I came to see that they were all very simple—lying in warm water, the smell of sweet olive blossoms in the air, the feel of clean sheets, or the sight of a hummingbird darting on my deck. From that foray came the book *Simple Pleasures: Soothing Suggestions and Small Comforts for Living Well Year-Round* in which my co-authors David Greer and Robert Taylor and I asked people what were the simple things that added delight and meaning to their lives.

In collecting the stories, I was struck by how often people spoke of gardening—both indoors and out—as one of the primary pleasures of their lives. I realized that without my being consciously aware of it, it was also true for me.

Some of my earliest memories relate to garden pleasures— the subtle smell of my mother's bearded iris, my father's yearly (always unsuccessful) attempt to get peaches from a tree his father grew from a seed in the ghetto of Boston, the taste of homegrown tomatoes, and freezing green beans in the steaming hot August kitchen. With the exception of my my father's peach failure, my parents both possess green thumbs. My mother is the kind of person who can put a pineapple top in a glass of water in her Cape Cod house, and not only will it grow, but it will flower and produce another pineapple! When I was growing up, gardening was simply the backdrop of my parents' lives, something I could participate in if I wanted to but with no obligation. Once I went away to college (my mother turned my bedroom into a plant room the day I left), I quickly acquired a host of houseplants and became one of the mainstay tenders of our commune's vegetable garden. I didn't even think about it; it just seemed like a natural part of life, like love and family.

Whether you're new to gardening or grew up with dirt under your fingernails, gardening offers a unique kind of pleasure. Perhaps it is its elemental nature. Daily life is so complex these days, but gardening can be so simple: put a seed in the ground, water it, and some day you will have a carrot. The results are so tangible—a rose bloom, an avocado tree, a philodendron that cascades down your office bookshelf. In the information age, so many of us do work that is so abstract; gardening is enormously satisfying because you can see the concrete results of your labor.

At a deeper level, for many of us, gardening is the one way we have to connect to nature on a regular basis. Even if you live at the top of the highest skyscraper with nary a tree in sight, your home can be filled with live green plants, and in tending them, you connect again, if only for a brief moment, to nature and thus to all that lives beyond human beings. For thousands of years, humans lived in close partnership with nature and, at some almost imperceptible level, we hunger for that connection still. Our fushsias and hydrangeas and moth orchids help fill the void left by the concretization of modern life.

Gardening can't help but put you in touch with the cycles of nature: Houseplants should be transplanted in late winter for spring's growth spurt, tomatoes must have the hot summer sun, and winter frost brings death to the vegetable garden. These are natural laws and, again, because we humans lived so long in harmony with such truths, there is great pleasure in aligning ourselves with those laws. Henry David Thoreau, the master of simple pleasures, suggests that we consciously "Live in each season as it passes: Breathe the air, drink the drink, taste the fruit, and resign yourself to the influences of each."

And so you will find *Simple Pleasures of the Garden* arranged seasonally to help us connect to the rhythms and cycles of natural life. The pleasures of each season are quite different: Spring, the season of new beginnings, is a very active time in the garden for pruning, preparing the soil, and starting seedlings. Summer is the time to really enjoy your garden, to crank up the barbeque, to sit outside on balmy evenings, to invite friends for candle-lit dinners on the patio, to enjoy the myriad perfumes your garden gives off, the summer garden is the place to relax and entertain. Fall pleasures are those of a more subtle variety—the harvesting of all your labors, the crisp tang in the air, and the sense of winding down. Winter is fantasy time—the time to hibernate inside, to plan for next year.

In each season, garden enjoyments are not restricted to the garden itself. Each season offers a chance to bring the garden indoors. That's why *Simple Pleasures of the Garden,* in addition to offering many stories by happy gardeners, gives a myriad of garden-related arts and crafts, recipes, and aromatherapy treats you can make yourself and enjoy with family and friends. I hope it inspires you to savor each precious moment and to find new delight in the simple, earthy pleasures that gardening can bring.

Spring

*Spring shows
what God can do
with a drab and dirty world.*

—Virgil A. Kraft

In the Garden

*In the dooryard fronting an old farm-house near
the white-wash'd palings,*

*Stands the lilac-bush tall frowing with heart-
shaped leaves of rich green,*

*With many a pointed blossom ringing delicate,
with the perfume strong I love,*

With every leaf a miracle...

—Walt Whitman

About to Blossom

One of my favorite times in my flower garden is pre-bloom time. The blush on the plant about to bloom starts to glow. It resembles a young girl of that certain age—twelve? thirteen?—just starting to fill out, grow up, straining to show her hidden promise. Then, a shine and dominance as it pushes everything out of the way to say, "Watch out world, here I come!" Tomorrow or the next day, I know it will be soon. Its arms reach out to the warm sun and soft spring rains. Everything surrounding it stays down and low, letting this one

In the Garden

have its turn in the sun. I await anxiously for the peak to arrive. Tomorrow?

One of the most delightful things about a garden
is the anticipation it provides.

—W. E. Johns

Signs of Spring

Nature signals the return of spring to each of us in a different way. For some, it is the blooming of a redbud or forsythia; for others, it is the determined daffodil, who is the trumpeter of spring, in bold pre-Easter yellow. For me, it is the dogwood tree, budding up everywhere with pink-infused blossoms of thickest cream. I love that the dogwood is such a democrat, growing anywhere and everywhere, in places where no other such beauty dare show herself.

A man ought to carry himself in the world as an
orange tree would if it could walk up and down
in the garden, swinging perfume from every little
censer it holds up in the air.

—Henry Ward Beecher

Wildflower Meadow

I don't know about you, but I believe a lawn is vastly overrated. It takes a tremendous amount of water, too much labor, and causes vast quantities of chemicals to be dumped into our water supply. So I decided to dig mine up and plant a wildflower meadow instead. It took some work to get going, but within four weeks I had my first bloom. It was a glorious sight for six months and unlike a lawn, virtually maintenance-free. Plus I had an almost endless supply of cut flowers from late spring to late fall.

The tricks are to till the soil in the spring, select a pure wildflower mix (no grass or vermiculite filler) appropriate to your growing area, and blend the seed with four times its volume of fine sand so it will disperse evenly. After you've spread it over the dirt, lay down a layer of loose hay to keep the seeds from blowing away. Usually the mixes are a combination of annuals, biannuals, and perennials. And to keep the annuals going, you have to rough up parts of the soil and reseed just those every year.

> *To be overcome by the fragrance of flowers is a delectable form of defeat.*
>
> —Beverley Nichols

In the Garden

The Way to a Woman's Heart is Through Her Nose

I have always been extremely sensitive to smells. Blessed (or cursed) by a finely tuned sense of smell, I find I am often led around by my nose. I have fallen in love because of the way a man smelled; when I was a child and my parents were away on a trip, I used to steal into their bathroom and smell their robes hanging on the back of the door. One of my favorite books is *Perfume,* the story of a man so affected by scents he can smell them from hundreds of miles away.

Naturally enough, I am attracted to flowers primarily for their scent. All my roses are chosen for odor—spicy-sweet, musky, peppery—if they don't smell good, I don't want them. My current favorite is a climber called Angel Face. I also love the heady smell of lavender, the spiciness of daffodils, the romance of lilacs and lilies of the valley, and the subtlety of certain beard-ed irises. I particularly love the elusiveness of fragrance. You catch a scent in the garden and follow your nose to...where? Now it's here; then it's gone. That's why I love the sweet olive tree that blooms in southern California in early spring. The fragrance is strong in the early evening as you walk down the street, but press your nose against a blossom and the scent diminishes.

My husband, who knows of my fragrant passion, surprised me last spring by planting me a huge patch of multicolored sweet peas and an entire bed of rubrum and Casablanca lilies. Batches of sweet peas perfumed my office throughout the spring. Extremely long-lasting as cut flowers, the lilies bloomed for two solid months during the summer and, all that time, the house was full of their heady scent. I don't think any gift has ever pleased me more.

> And because the breath of flowers is far sweeter
> in the air (where it comes and goes,
>
> like the warbling of music) than in the hand,
> therefore nothing is more fit for that delight
>
> than to know what be the flowers and plants that
> do best perfume the air.
>
> —Francis Bacon

Fragrant Plants

Smell is so individual—I love narcissus, but know many people who can't stand it, and folks wax eloquent about wisteria, the smell of which makes me sick. So in creating a fragrant garden, let your nose be your guide. Here are some suggestions: jasmine, honeysuckle, sweet autumn clematis, mimosa, hosta,

In the Garden

stock, evening primrose, nicotana, angel trumpet (especially the white), moonflower, sweet pea, ginger, lily of the valley, peony, and pinks.

> *Working in the garden gives me something*
> *beyond the enjoyment of senses. It gives me a*
> *profound feeling of inner peace.*
>
> —Ruth Stout

My Primrose Patch

As a young girl, I was particularly taken by a row of primroses my mother had in a border planting. The colors were deep and pure like my favorite crayons—purplish blues, intense red-orange, and buttery yellows. I loved that such beauty came up out of a rather commonplace and cabbagey foliage. When Mom showed me how to carefully separate the "babies" from the established adult primroses, I planted my very own in my favorite mysterious blue in "my" part of the garden. Mom, who ran a small but busy dairy farm, also showed me her secrets of accelerating plant growth, without the blue hormone-filled potions you could buy at the hardware store. (That was cheating in her book.) She would take well "cured" cow dung and mix it into the soil around her plants. I took her cue, and by the next spring I had a prim little row of primroses that had all sprung from the baby I had brought home and transplanted. It was at that point that my mom nodded approvingly and I was pronounced to have a green thumb.

> *One of the daintiest joys of spring is the falling of*
> *soft rain among blossoms.*
>
> —Mary Webb

A Flower Bed

I found an old bed in a neighbor's trash. It was too pretty to be thrown away. It had only the foot and headboard. I set them at each end of a row of flowers in one of my gardens. When a passerby asks me why the bed is in the middle of my garden, I reply with, "Haven't you ever heard of a flower bed?" I now have a herb bed too. I'm looking for an old crib to set around my seedlings, and that will be my nursery bed.

> *The first gathering of salads, radishes and herbs*
> *made me feel like a mother about her baby—how*
> *could anything so beautiful be mine?*
>
> —Alice B. Toklas

In the Garden

The Boldness of Tulips

I love tulips better than any other spring flower: They are the embodiment of alert cheerfulness and tidy grace, and next to a hyacinth they look like wholesome, freshly scrubbed young girls beside stout ladies whose every movement weights down the air with patchouli. Their faint, delicate scent is refinement itself; and is there anything in the world more charming than the sprightly way they hold up their little faces to the sun? I have heard them called bold and flaunting. But to me they seem modest grace itself, only always on the alert to enjoy life as much as they can and not afraid of looking the sun or anything else above them in the face.

> *To dig one's own spade into one's own earth! Has*
> *life anything better to offer than this?*
>
> —Beverley Nichols

The Pleasure of Sound

I f you want a more sophisticated sound for your garden than wind chimes normally offer, consider garden bells. They are a set of cup shaped metal bells on wires that come with a base. Like chimes, they peal when blown by the breeze. Unlike chimes, however, the tones change when they are filled with rain, and their sound can be adjusted by bending the wires. Call Woodstock Percussion, (800-422-4463).

> *And all it lends to the sky is this—*
> *A sunbeam giving the air a kiss.*
>
> —Harry Kemp,
> "The Hummingbird"

A Spring Reverie

*I*n the enclosure, the spring flowers are almost too beautiful— a great stretch of foamlike cowslips. As I bend over them, the air is heavy and sweet with their scent, like hay and new milk and the kisses of children, and, further on, a sunlit wonder of chiming daffodils.

Before me are two great rhododendron bushes. Against the dark, broad leaves the blossoms rise, flame-like, tremulous in the still air, and the pear rose loving-cup of a magnolia hands delicately on the grey bough.

In the Garden

> *May all your weeds be wildflowers.*
>
> —Gardening plaque

For Love of Weeds

As I work in my vegetable garden, tenderly planting seedlings of peppers, cucumbers, and tomatoes, I suddenly spot the weeds and regretfully rip them out by their roots. Regretfully, because I'm a great fan of weeds. Weeds are the wonder workers of the world. Weeds covered the hellhole of Hiroshima with a living green carpet of hope. Within a year after the volcanic explosion, weeds brightened the miles of volcanic ash around Mount St. Helen's. As I stood in Yellowstone disconsolately peering at a desolate forest of giants blacked by the great fire, my eye fastened on small clumps of green—patches of weeds whispering on the winds, "we will be back."

Rain in spring is as precious as oil.

—Chinese proverb

Surprise Guests

I strive to be an urban gardener but rarely do much better than a pot of basil and a few annuals in my window boxes. However, I discovered a toil-free pleasure in my back patio. Since we live in an older building, there are a bunch of old planters filled with dirt and scruffy remnants of plants. One day I decided to water these planters and was pleasantly rewarded a week or so later with a profusion of mostly weeds but some flowers. One box even yielded a red tulip this spring. Even the weeds are pretty though' and one bunch has tiny orange flowers on spindly branches. All it took was a little time and a little water. I enjoy the daily anticipation as new things reveal themselves, and, besides, it's far prettier than the brown scruffy stuff.

> *To win the secret of a weed's plain heart.*
>
> —James Russell Lowell

Produce for Apartment Dwellers

*I*f you have no space or time for a garden (or are plagued by critters eating your goodies before you get to them), try creating hanging vegetable baskets. According to experts, almost anything can be grown in a basket, but be sure to get compact growing varieties of the vegetables you want. Buy 14-inch diameter wire baskets (16-inch for zucchini or watermelons). It's best to grow one type of vegetable per basket, although a variety of lettuces or herbs will work well together.

In the Garden

Line with sphagnum moss and fill with potting soil. Plant seedlings rather than seeds, and hang the baskets outdoors from patios or rafters where they will get at least four hours of afternoon sun. Avoid overwatering seedlings, but once they become established, be aware you need to feed and water frequently; on the hottest days, they may even need to be watered twice a day! Once seedlings are three weeks old, fertilize every three weeks with an all-purpose soluble fertilizer, but never feed unless the soil is damp.

> *To be beautiful and to be calm, without mental*
> *fear, is the ideal of nature.*
>
> —Richard Jefferies

Easy Care Gardening

*T*oo busy to care for a vegetable garden on your own or don't have the room? Consider what 100,000 folks around the United States do—"buy" shares in someone's large garden. All shareholders agree to pay a certain amount per year and, in exchange, get weekly baskets of produce. Depending on where you live, deliveries can be anywhere from twenty–two to fifty–two weeks per year.

Like most good ideas, this one has a name—Community Supported Agriculture—and an organization, CSANA. According to CSANA, shares usually cost between 300 and 600 dollars per year. (Many offer discounts for labor; since the work is shared, no one is overburdened, and there's the added bonus of meeting fellow gardeners you might not otherwise know.) For more information about the 600 farms that belong to CSANA, contact them at (413-528-4374) or e-mail to csana@bcn.net. Their web address is http://www.umass.edu/umext/CSA.

> *I am not…certain that I want to be able to iden-*
> *tify all the warblers. There is a charm sometimes*
> *in not knowing what or who the singer is.*
>
> —Donald Culross Peattie

Remembering Lilacs

I suppose the garden behind my grandparents house was small, but to a four-year-old it seemed immense. The distance from the backdoor to the end of the yard was a journey from the safety of home, across an expanse of grass, around orderly flower beds, and finally to the marvelous wilderness of the tall, old lilac hedge. I discovered that a persistent push would let me enter a cool, green space under the branches of the lilacs. There I daily established my first household, presiding over tea parties for an odd assortment of stuffed animals and the patient family cat.

In the Garden

Now, nearly seven decades later, the heady scent of lilacs takes me back to that garden where I took those first ventures toward independence—though never out of sight of the familiar backdoor.

> *Unless the soul goes out to meet what we see we*
> *do not see it; nothing do we see, not a beetle, not*
> *a blade of grass.*
>
> —William Henry Hudson

Public Gardening

*L*onging for a garden but have no place for one? Take advantage of the variety of places that have gardens: zoos, public gardens and parks, cemeteries, college campuses, garden club tours, nurseries and garden centers, or a friend's house. In many cities these days, there are also community gardens and gardening coops in which you can get your hands dirty. Call your parks and recreation department. (All of the above are also great places to get ideas if you do have a garden.)

> *The only conclusion I have ever reached is that I*
> *love all trees, but I am in love with pines.*
>
> —Aldo Leopold

Butterfly Haven

*I*f you want to increase the butterfly population in your yard, there's a wide variety of flowers that will attract them, including common yarrow, New York aster, Shasta daisy, coreopsis, horsemint, lavender, rosemary, thyme, butterfly bush, shrubby cinquefoil, common garden petunia, verbena, pincushion flowers, cosmos, zinnia, globe amaranth, purple coneflower, sunflowers, lupine, delphinium. In creating a butterfly-friendly place, consider that they also need wind protection, a quiet place to lay eggs, and water to drink.

If you want to see a butterfly garden before you get started, many botanical societies have them. In Washington, D.C., the Smithsonian just opened one adjacent to the National Museum of Natural History. Good guides include: *The Butterfly Garden* by Matthew Tekulsky (Harvard Common Press) or *Butterfly Gardening* by Xerces Society/Smithsonian Institution (Sierra Club Books).

> *I believe a leaf of grass is no less than the*
> *journey-work of the stars,*
> *And the pismire is equally perfect, and*
> *a grain of sand, and the egg of the wren,*
> *And the tree-toad is a chef-d'oeuvre for*

In the Garden

the highest,
And the runny blackberry would
adorn the parlors of heaven
And the narrowest hinge in my hand
puts to scorn all machinery,
And the cow crunching with depress'd
head surpasses any statue,
And a mouse is miracle enough to
stagger sextillions of infidels.

—Walt Whitman

With Family and Friends

All God's pleasures are simple ones; the rapture of a May morning sunshine, the stream blue and green, kind words, benevolent acts, the glow of good humor.

—F. W. Robertson

The Wonders of Wildflowers

My mother is a naturalist at heart. She treasures wildflowers much more than the domesticated plants I adopted as a child. She would take me on wildflower walks and teach me the secret flora of meadow and wood. I learned to identify wild irises, jack-in-the-pulpit, Dutchman's breeches, larkspur, lady's slippers, and dozens of gorgeous and delicate specimens. I wondered at the difference between the small and seemingly rare wildflowers and the big and bold flowers that grew in our garden. The irises especially were in great contrast—wild irises were about four inches high and the irises I started from my aunt's were over two feet tall.

One day, I decided to surprise my mother by transplanting some of her treasured wild irises to a flower bed at home. She

With Family
& Friends

was pleased, but warned me that these delicate plants simply wouldn't thrive outside their habitat. By the next spring, however, we had hearty clump of wild irises growing beside the shameless "flags" from Auntie's house.

> *They tell us that plants are perishable, soulless creatures, that only man is immortal, but this, I think, is something that we know very nearly nothing about.*
>
> —John Muir

Bringing the Woods Home

*T*here are a number of woodland flowers that will do well in any shaded and treed part of your yard with moist, well-drained, rich-in-humus soil (you can add your own peat moss if you need to). These include lily of the valley (my personal favorite), dog's tooth violet, great trillium, red trillium, false Solomon's seal, Virginia bluebells, and redwood sorrel. But beware—don't just go digging up plants in the woods; many, such as lady's slipper and swamp pink, are endangered. Better to get them from a reputable (some suppliers of difficult-to-propagate plants are overcollecting from the wild) company such as Prairie Moon Nursery (send $2 to Rt. 2, Box 163, Winona, MN

55987 for a catalog), Underwood Shade Gardens (508-222-2164, $4 for catalog), and Shady Oaks Nursery (800-504-8006, $4 for catalog).

> *Each flower is a soul opening out to nature.*
>
> —Gerard de Nerval

Mother's Day Sachet

Here's something middle-school kids can make mom or grandmom for Mother's Day.

¼ yard lace

1 dinner plate

disappearing ink marker

scissors

1 cereal bowl

tapestry needle

2 yards ¼" wide wired ribbon

2 ounces lavender or potpourri

2 yards 1" wide ribbon

Place the lace on a table and lay the dinner plate on top of it. Trace the edge of the plate with the disappearing ink marker. Remove plate and cut around marker to make a circle of lace. Turn the cereal bowl upside down in the center of the lace circle and trace the edge. Remove bowl.

With Family & Friends

Thread the tapestry needle with the thin ribbon and stitch around the inner circle you have just created. (Size of stitches doesn't matter.) Tug gently on the ribbon so the lace gathers to make a pocket. When the opening is the size of a silver dollar, pour the lavender or potpourri in until full (about the size of a walnut). Tug the ribbon tight, tie in a knot, and cut the ends short.

Tie the wide ribbon into a beautiful bow. Repeat until materials are gone. Makes 5 sachets.

Seeds of Wonder

*K*ids love to help in the garden. It's a wonderful place for a child to learn and have fun and to spend enjoyable time with you. As you are starting to prepare your garden this spring, consider setting aside a special plot or container specifically for them. Pick plants that will grow quickly (patience is short) and those that have personality (like the face in a pansy); fragrance; texture (like lamb's ears); vibrant color; and/or attract butterflies. Good options depending on space and climate are: Chinese lantern, columbine, pinks, poppies, stock, sunflower, cornflower, bachelor's button, cosmos, violas, snapdragons, and zinnias. Take the kids with you to the nursery, and let them select from the above choices.

You can also help youngsters sprout seeds indoors. Fold a couple of paper towels together to form a strip as wide as the towel and a few inches high. Moisten and place inside a peanut butter jar or similar-size jar, forming a border at the base. Crumple and moisten another paper towel and stuff into the center. Carefully place seeds—beans are easy to grow and handle—between the folded paper and the glass. Keep moist, but not soaked, for several days as seeds germinate. Kids can watch roots and plants sprout. When plants reach above the jar and two sets of leaves have formed, transplant to pots of soil or into the ground.

If you want kid-sized tools and more suggestions as to how to involve kids in gardening, now there is a company that specializes in garden supplies for kids as well as tools, games, and books for backyard nature study: Gardens for Growing People. They also feature gardening course curriculums for teachers. For a free catalog, call (415-663-9433). To subscribe to their newsletter, e-mail them at growpepl@nbn.com.

> *Every happening, great and small, is a parable*
> *whereby God speaks to us and the art of life is to*
> *get the message.*
>
> —Malcolm Muggeridge

*With Family
& Friends*

Heartful Greens

One easy way to entice your child into the garden is to make a patch with their name. Simply trace out his or her name in the loose soil and trace a big heart around it. Then plant a variety of fast-growing greens (leaf lettuce, radishes, watercress, arugula) in the furrows made by your tracings, water, and wait for his or her name and a big green heart to appear. Chances are your little one will not only enjoy helping, but he or she will eat salad too!

I have always thought a kitchen garden a
more pleasant sight than the finest orangery or
artificial greenhouse.

—Joseph Addison

Gather Thee Rose Petals

When I was young, my brother and sister and I used to make May baskets for all the houses in the neighborhood to celebrate May Day. They were incredibly easy to make, and we would get such a thrill out of hanging them on front-door knobs, then ringing the bell and running to a hiding spot where we would observe the face of the recipient. It was then I first learned the particular pleasure of anonymous giving. It's been a long time since I even thought about it, but the remembered pleasure is so strong, I think I'll do it with my kids this spring.

A flower is an educated weed.

—Luther Burbank

May Baskets

*T*o make yourself or your neighbors a May basket, gather flowers (we always picked the first wildflowers of the season, but store-bought are okay too) and make them into an attractive bouquet. Tie the stems together with a rubber band. Moisten half a paper towel with water and wrap around the ends of the stem and then place a small plastic bag around the towel and tie with another rubber band. (This is to keep flowers fresh.) Set aside.

To make a cone basket, get a 8½ x 11-inch piece of construction paper. Hold the paper in two hands as if you were reading a letter. Turn slightly so that the left corner points down at you. This will be the bottom of the cone. Roll one side so that it is tighter at bottom and more open at top. Stick your hand in top to expand the top opening and at the same time tighten the point at the bottom. Staple or tape the outer flap. When you finish, it should look like an ice cream waffle cone. To make the

With Family & Friends

handle, simply cut a ½-inch wide strip from the long side of a 8½-x-11-inch piece of construction paper. Staple one end to each side of the cone. (You can also use ribbon or raffia if you want to.) Place flowers inside and you are ready to make your delivery!

> *The garden is a love song, a duet between a human being and Mother Nature.*
>
> —Jeff Cox

Plant Passalongs

*M*y husband and I have green thumbs and it can get to be somewhat of a problem. Our houseplants never die and we are constantly having to pinch and hack them back. We feel guilty over just throwing all those potential new plants into the compost, so we are always rooting something. As large as our house is, we're running out of room. I take plants into the office, but that's also getting overpopulated.

Recently, however, we have come across several nonplant people eager to get started and therefore happy to take a number of cuttings off our hands. Most of these folks are young (probably because you are either a plant person or not as time goes on). We've given them as college graduation presents, first house presents, and new relationship presents. We always include fertilizer and instructions, and we always try to give plants appropriate to the light levels in the person's abode. Because this was a great solution to a "problem" of ours, it's been surprising to realize how pleasurable it is to start someone off on an interest in plants. They seem so happy; I recall my own first houseplant forays, and I'm left with a satisfied glow that no other gift-giving has ever provided.

> *The music of the night insects has been familiar*
> *to every generation of men since the earliest*
> *humans; it has come down like a Greek chorus*
> *chanting around the actors throughout the course*
> *of human history.*
>
> —Edwin Way Teale

Plant Propagation

Early spring is the best time to make new houseplants. There are four ways plant propagate, ranging from easy to hard (I for one refuse to do air layering), and some plants respond only to one or the other.

With Family & Friends

1. Division: You just take the plant out of the pot, divide it into two or more clumps, roots and all, and replant into two or more pots. Plants that do well with this

method include African violets, wax begonias, most ferns, agapanthus, and many orchids.

2. Offshoots and Runners: Plants such as spider plants, strawberry geranium, and mother fern create ready-made babies complete with tiny roots as appendages that are considered runners. Bromeliad's, clivia's, and piggyback plant's offspring grow adjacent to the mother. In either case, I just detach the baby and plant it in a tiny pot out of direct sun, giving it plenty of moisture. (With runners, there's a way to do it while it is still attached to the plant, but that's too much work for me.)

3. Stem cuttings: My mainstay. Simply cut off a stem, strip off lower leaves, and place in water. (Don't touch the surface of the cut—bacteria from your skin can make the stem rot.) In a month or so, it will have rooted and you can transplant it into a pot. Avoid rot by placing a couple charcoal chips at the bottom of the container. Many houseplants will root this way including: coleus, fuschia, philodendron, Swedish ivy, Miniature rose, pothos, and wandering Jew. For cactus and succulents, let the cuttings dry for at least 24 hours and root in rooting medium such as perlite or vermiculite.

4. Air layering: Required for dieffenbachia, dracena, ficus and split-leave philodendron. To find out how to do this, ask at your local nursery.

Flowers preach to us if we will hear.

—Christina Rossetti

Plant Swapping

*U*sually passing along plants is a two-person exchange, but it is possible to set up a larger-scale swap. You could perhaps do it through your local agricultural co-op or set something up like a flea market or garage sale. Run an ad in the classifieds and tell all the garden club people in your community. I know of one group in Texas that had 200 people show up! All you need are tables and a few rules. Here's how the Texas folks do it: They hold it in a place that can stand the dirt, require that the donated plant be a "good" one—no unrooted cuttings, seeds, diseased plants, etc.—and limit the number of plants you can bring to swap. They ask people to label the plants they bring and include care instructions (Sun? Perennial? Drought Tolerant? Indoor?) As people bring in plants, the plants are given a number and a corresponding slip of paper with the same number goes into a hat. Then the hat is passed around and you get the plant with the corresponding number. After that, people mill around trying to trade if they don't like their plants or get cuttings from the plants they lust over. If you have a smaller crowd, of course you can just have people barter

With Family & Friends

between themselves for the plants they want and skip the numbers. Either way, the purpose is to have fun, mingle with plant people, and go home with something new.

> *And this our life, exempt from public haunt*
> *Finds tongues in trees, books in running brooks,*
> *Sermons in stones and good in every thing.*
>
> —William Shakespeare

Into the Kitchen

Every thing is good in its season.

—Italian proverb

Ode to Asparagus

*T*he ancients believe that asparagus was an aphrodisiac. It certainly tastes good enough to be, but even if it isn't, the prospect of your own tender shoots each spring should entice you enough to give it a try in your garden. It takes about three years to get enough asparagus to make planting it worthwhile, but a maintained asparagus bed will last for twenty years, so you'll get plenty of spears for your efforts. While asparagus prefers cold winters, it will grow just about anywhere in the U.S. The trick is to dig a one-foot-deep trench and half fill it with compost and ¼ cup bone meal per one foot of trench. Plant roots 18 inches apart, and don't fill in trench with dirt until roots begin to sprout.

Into the Kitchen

Green fingers are the extensions of a verdant heart.

—Russell Page

Stir-Fried Asparagus

Once you've grown them and had your fill of steamed, give this a try. It is delicious!

2 tablespoons low-sodium soy sauce

1 tablespoon dry sherry

1 tablespoon water or chicken broth

1 tablespoon sesame oil

1½ pounds asparagus, ends snapped, and cut into small pieces

2 teaspoons minced garlic

2 teaspoons minced fresh ginger

½ cup minced fresh basil

½ teaspoon sugar

Combine the soy sauce, sherry, and water or broth and set aside. Place a large (at least 12-inch) skillet over high heat for 4 minutes. Add 2 teaspoons of the oil and heat for 1 minute or until the oil just starts to smoke. Add the asparagus and stir-fry for about 2 minutes or until barely tender. Clear the center of the pan, add the garlic, ginger, and 1 teaspoon of oil, saute for 10 seconds. Remove pan from heat and stir the ingredients to combine.

Place pan back on heat, stir in the soy sauce mixture, and cook for 30 seconds. Add basil and sugar and cook for another 30 seconds. Serves 4.

A Humble Root

*I*n his book *Tomato Blessings and Radish Teachings,* Zen cook and teacher Edward Espe Brown ruminates on the lessons food has to offer. Here he is attending a dinner party and describes the appetizer: "Radishes! Seated at a low table, we came face to face with platters of radishes, brilliantly red and curvaceous, some elongated and white tipped, rootlets intact with topknots of green leaves sprouting from the opposite end. It was love at first sight. Gazing at the plentitude of radishes, red and round with narrow roots and spreading stems, I felt a swelling joy.... these radishes kept growing on me, as if they exuded happiness.... To be able to see the virtue, to appreciate the goodness of simple, unadorned ingredients—this is probably the primary task of the cook."

> *Sow the living part of yourselves in the furrow of life.*
>
> —Miguel de Unamino

Lettuce Entertain You

Into the Kitchen

*E*ach year, the average American household consumes 27.6 pounds of lettuce, most of it the iceberg variety (although with Caesar salads a staple of so many restaurant menus, romaine must be a close second.) Why not break out of the rut? Bon Vivant, Royal Red, Monet, and Lollo Rosso Atsina are all gourmet leaf varieties worth considering. Check out seed catalogs from Vermont Bean (802-273-3400), J. W. Jung Seed (414-326-3121), and Sumway (803-663-9771).

Fresh Herb Salad

This is a salad from Provence that uses an unusual variety of late-spring greens and herbs.

1 garlic cloves, halved

2 teaspoons lemon juice

$\frac{1}{4}$ teaspoon salt

4 teaspoons olive oil

1 teaspoon hot water

4 cups arugula

1-2 cups watercress, large stems removed

1 $\frac{1}{2}$ cups escarole

$\frac{1}{4}$ cup parsley, stems removed

$\frac{1}{2}$ cup curly endive

$\frac{1}{4}$ cup small basil leaves

20 small tarragon leaves

10 small sage leaves

5 chives, minced

pepper

Rub the garlic clove halves all over a large wooden salad bowl. Whisk in the lemon, salt, olive oil, and water. Add greens and pepper to taste. Serve immediately. Serves 4.

Picking Volunteers

My city-born husband was at my southern mother's house with me one year when she remarked that she felt like cooking a pot of "volunteers." After enjoying his confused expression for a few seconds, I explained that this is what she calls the small patch of turnip greens that come up every year without any coaxing or invitation. So we headed out to pick a mess, and I schooled him on how to pick the small tender leaves and to pick quickly so as to avoid the scratchy texture of the plants. He didn't care much for the greens, but I do think he enjoyed the picking.

> *Anywhere you live you can find room for a garden somewhere.*
>
> —Jamie Jobb

Into the Kitchen

Forgotten Vegetables

*B*esides turnip greens there are many other vegetables that seem to be overlooked in the typical American diet. Recent research comparing French and American diets found that the French eat three times the variety of vegetables that we do and the variety alone may have healthful benefits. So why not consider the following for your garden this summer?

Chard: red or green, can be eaten raw when the leaves are tender, or used like cabbage to make chard rolls. Also good for a winter pasta sauce.

Kale: member of cabbage family, popular among Romans and Greeks, loaded with vitamins and never bitter. Superb steamed.

Kohlrabi: turnip-like root with edible stems. Can be eaten raw like an apple, shredded like a cabbage, or cooked like a turnip.

Amaranth: also known as Chinese spinach. Rich in iron, calcium, vitamin A. Cook like spinach or chard.

Good King Henry: also known as poor man's asparagus. Leaves and shoots can be cooked like spinach.

Purslane: can be used in salads or cooked like spinach. Sharp tasting, but high in vitamin C and omega-3 fatty acids that help prevent heart problems.

Popping Fresh Corn

You can grow your own popping corn. One of the most fun varieties is Pretty Pops, which has kernels of red, blue, orange, black, purple, and yellow. Left on the cob, its great for decorating your home. And it's wonderful tasting when popped (kernels turn white though).

> *It's the leisure hours, happily used, that have*
> *opened up a new world to many a person.*
>
> —George M. Adams

Red Hot Mamas

If you like spicy food, consider growing a variety of hot peppers this summer. Recently scientists have found the substance that creates the heat in peppers. It's called capsaicin, an antioxidant that gives chilies their bite and, like all antioxidants, may help prevent cancer.

Some chili peppers, rated from low to high capsaicin content (and therefore amount of "heat"), are

Into the Kitchen

New Mexico red: (rated 2–3)

jalapeno: 5

serrano: 6

Tabasco: 8

Thai: 9

Scotch Bonnet: 10

savina: 10+

A variety of chili seeds are available from Shepard's Garden Seeds (860-482-3638) and Native Seeds/SEARCH (520-327-9123). Already grown chilies of various sorts are available from Stonewall Chili Pepper (800-232-2995) and Penzeys Ltd. (414-574-0277).

> *There is something about sun and soil that heals*
> *broken bodies and jangled nerves.*
>
> —Nature magazine

Garden in a Jar

*T*he very first garden I remember was a sweet potato in a jar. My mama planted it when we were living in three tiny rooms behind our dress shop. There was no yard, no room outside even for a flowerpot. But Mama filled a Mason jar with water, propped the long, skinny sweet potato up in the glass with a trio of toothpicks, and told my brother and me to watch.

By summer, the kitchen window was curtained with graceful vines and big curving leaves. And somehow that window garden made our shabby little kitchen into a special place. Even the light seemed different—more restful, more alive.

That was when I first realized I needed a garden in my life.

> *What I know of the divine sciences and the Holy*
> *Scriptures, I learned in woods and fields. I have*
> *no other masters than the beeches and the oaks.*
>
> —St. Bernard of Clairvaux

Into the Kitchen

Beautifying Your Home

*Now the earth with many flowers puts on her
spring embroidery.*

—Sappho

Gathering Moss

*T*o add a distinctive look to outdoor pots and planters, try this simple trick: Create a mixture containing one part garden soil, two parts peat moss, and one part water—the mixture should be gooey and thick in consistency. Using a garden trowel or your hand, spread the exterior of a terra cotta pot or planter with the mixture, and allow to dry. Sow seeds or outdoor plantings as desired in the pots, and water normally. Within a few weeks, the peat moss mixture will have blossomed with a variety of mosses and lichens, giving your pots a verdant, natural patina.

*Growing a garden and staying out in the fresh air
after office hours seemed to give me the strength
to meet all problems with greater courage.*

—Jim G. Brown

Beautifying Your
Home

Mintcense

One thing you can do if you decide to grow a variety of mint is to make mint potpourri. Originally made in colonial times, when it was believed to "clear the head," it is an excellent natural room freshener. From a recipe by Phyllis Shaudys, who says the concoction sells well at craft fairs.

½ cup orris root

1 tablespoon oil of lavender or pennyroyal

2 cups dried orange mint

2 cups dried spearmint

2 cups dried peppermint

1 cup dried thyme

1 cup dried rosemary

Combine the orris root and essential oil. Add the rest of the ingredients and combine gently, taking care not to crush the leaves too much. Store in a covered jar. To use, shake and open.

Natural Moth Repellants

If you want to avoid moth balls for your woolens this coming summer, try dried branches of rue, tansy, mint, lavender, rosemary, pennyroyal, and wormwood either by themselves or in combination. Tie them together and, to avoid them flaking onto your closet floor, wrap them lightly in cheesecloth and hang upside down from a ribbon in your closet.

> *A house, though otherwise beautiful, yet if it hath*
> *no garden is more like a prison than a house.*
>
> —William Coles

Naturally Dyed Easter Eggs

Want to do something a little more sophisticated this Easter? You and your older kids might enjoy the subtle beauty of these natural wonders. But be aware—these are for decoration only. Do not eat.

1 red cabbage

3 very large brown-skinned onions

1 dozen eggs

36 rubber bands

2 dozen small fern fronds and/or fresh and dried flower blossoms

1 tablespoon powdered alum

1 roll cheesecloth

Beautifying Your Home

Without cutting the cabbage in two, cut the central core out and separate the leaves so that each leaf is as large as possible.

Cut the two ends off the onions and peel the skin off, again keeping each piece of skin as large as possible.

Place a fern or flower against an egg on either side and wrap it completely with a red cabbage leaf, using two rubber bands to keep it on. Repeat for five more eggs. Use the onion skins and remaining flowers and ferns for the other six eggs, again using two rubber bands to affix. Cut 12 pieces of cheesecloth big enough to wrap completely around each egg and secure with two more rubber bands.

Place the cabbage eggs in one pot and the onion eggs in another. Add water and 1½ teaspoon alum to each pot. Bring to a boil, reduce heat, and simmer for 15 minutes. Remove from heat and allow eggs to cool in water. Unwrap and enjoy your designs. Makes 1 dozen.

The hours when the mind is absorbed by beauty
are the only hours when we really live...

—Richard Jefferies

Eggshell Planters

Ordinary eggshells make beautiful planters for small herbs or grasses. Break raw eggs, leaving shell at least one-half intact. Empty the contents into a separate bowl, and rinse the shell thoroughly. Place already sprouting plants (mint, lavender, chives, or sage work well, as will wheatgrass, alfalfa, or small ferns) in the shells, anchored with a bit of topsoil. Cushion an assortment of shells and plants in moss, and place in a beribboned basket or pot. Experiment with using dyed or decorated egg shells.

Brighten Up!

Forego the typical white, and paint your garden furniture an unusual color. Look to nature for inspiration and realize that the wildest of color seems ordinary in a lovely garden. I just painted two Adirondack chairs bright celery green, and what was garish in the paint can look perfectly at ease in my garden.

> *May my life be like a great hospitable tree, and*
> *may weary wanderers find in me a rest.*
>
> —John Henry Jowett

Water Gardens

It seems that garden ponds are in these days; the garden catalogs are full of such kits. I even have a friend who had an

Beautifying Your Home

entire stream put in his property. I must say when I saw it, I lusted after it myself until I realized the trouble and expense it would take. One day I read an article by the horticulturalist for the Denver Botanic Gardens in which he sang the praises of tiny water gardens. They are easy to create, hard to goof on (you can always rearrange), and—as long as you have a location that gets six hours of sun—the plants are hard to kill. So I decided to give it a try. Mine is made out of one of those nine-inch black plastic containers that look like they're cast iron. All it has is a tiny cattail, a spider lily, and a clump of cranberry taro. It sits in the middle of my vegetable garden, and I smile every time I see it.

To live happily is an inward power of the soul.

—Marcus Aurelius

Making a Mini-Pond

All it takes is a water-tight container and a few plants. You can use half barrels, if you line them with PVC liner (available at garden centers), or ceramic pots, as long as you seal them with two coats of sealant. Plastic pots require no preparation. Use plants with contrasting shapes to create an appealing design, but don't use too many different ones; you're working in a small space and too much variety will look chaotic. And remember—they will grow, so take that into account in your design. You just submerge the pot, dirt and all, into the water. You can get height differentials by setting the plants on submerged bricks or overturned pots. Good water plants include water lettuce, water hyacinth, sweet flag, parrot feather, cannas, calla lilies, giant arrowhead, yellow pitcher plant, and water celery. Fertilize with pellets available at any nursery. If you live in a place that freezes, bring the plants in to use as houseplants for the winter or keep them in a tub of water in the basement. They most likely will need to be divided in the spring. Start another pond or give the new ones away.

> *We are not sent into this world to do anything into which we cannot put our hearts.*
>
> —John Ruskin

Sand Lamps

When the weather starts to turn warm and you want to hold an evening garden party, consider this easy-to-make lighting. Simply buy some beautiful terra-cotta pots (or use the ones your plants have grown out of, but make sure they are terra-cotta, not plastic). Make a plug of masking tape over the drain hole, fill with sand and insert a fat candle. Shield the

Beautifying Your Home

candle from the wind with hurricane-lamp chimneys, available at home improvement and import stores such as Pier One and Cost Plus.

> *Awake, O north wind, and come thou south!*
> *Blow upon my garden,*
> *that the spices thereof may flow out...*
>
> —Song of Solomon

Nourishing Body and Soul

My faith is all a doubtful thing,
Wove on a doubtful loom,
Until there comes, each showery spring,
A cherry tree in bloom.

—David Morton

The Garden Grows You

Several years ago, I was walking in March along a gravel road that led to the ocean in Rhode Island. A very old and very thin woman came hobbling down a driveway towards me. I waved and continued walking, but as I passed, she grabbed my arm, turned around and began to pull me in the direction of her house. I instantly thought of the witch in *Hansel and Gretel,* and tried to pull back, but that only made her clutch tighter around my wrist. Besides, she didn't cackle, so I relented.

She didn't say a word, in fact, until we approached her house: a shingle-style cottage with green shutters and a front lawn erupting everywhere in purple crocus. She released me there, throwing her arms up in the air and shouting, "Look at this splendor! Isn't it a miracle?!"

*Nourshing Body
& Soul*

I didn't know what to say. I mean the crocus were every-where and indeed they were beautiful, but a miracle? Besides I had a very important problem I had been thinking about when she interrupted me and. . . .

Betts threw her arms around me. She smelled like earth and onions, rain and soap. She whispered in my ear, "You don't understand. As you grow a garden, it grows you!"

After that, I visited Betts Wodehouse every chance I could. It turned out she was a famous sculptress. Her mother had been friends with Rodin. She had letters from him in her study, but I never went inside Betts' house. We always went directly to her garden. At 90 or so, it was hard for her to bend down and weed, so I'd do it for her. One day she talked on and on about this weed that had spread everywhere and couldn't be pulled out without also taking some of the healthy plants. I realized later, she was also telling me she had incurable cancer.

Each time we were together, she taught me about gardening, but when I arrived home, I knew she had also been offering me lessons of the soul, lessons to nourish my dream seeds, espe-cially the twisted ones. As I would walk away down that gravel driveway, she'd always call to me, "Don't forget, as you grow your garden, your garden grows you!"

What was paradise but a Garden?

—William Coles

Elderflower Skin Refresher

If you live in an area where elderflowers grow, here's an old-fashioned skin tonic. This is a great gift when packaged in a beautiful glass bottle decorated with an old botanical illustration of an elderflower. Be sure to include storage instructions.

50 elderflower heads, washed in cold water

1 quart jar, sterilized

2$\frac{1}{2}$ cups water

5 tablespoons vodka

cheesecloth

decorative glass bottles with lids

Remove petals from heads, making sure not to bruise the flowers; do not include stems. Place petals in quart jar. Boil water and pour over flowers. Let stand for 30 minutes and add vodka. Cover and let stand on counter for 24 hours.

Pour liquid through cheesecloth into glass bottles and cap. Store in refrigerator until used. Then keep in cool, dry, dark place like a cabinet and use within one month. Makes 3 cups.

Nourshing Body & Soul

A Longing for Love

I was awakened around 5:30 one morning by a wonderful, trilling melody. Jumping up to find out what it was, I spied the tiniest wren singing his heart out. He was perched on a little tree branch just in front of a small birdhouse I had installed in my garden. This magical music kept up all day as I went about my business nearby in the garden. The little bird would take off and return to the branch with a wee bit of something in his beak. Is he making a nest? I wondered. This kept up for two days as I went about my daily routine, the little wren singing his heart out, seemingly searching "for what says I."

On the fourth day, lo and behold, there was the same beautiful notes from this tiniest of birds—but did I notice more activity? Yes, my faithful little wren had found his mate. Naturally the "for rent" sign was gone from the house. Now I will watch and wait for the little feathered arrivals. Such an exciting love story to watch unfold as I worked in my garden!

> *Your job as gardener is to try to keep things*
> *running smoothly for the plants and animals that*
> *live in or visit your yard, whatever the weather*
> *decides to do.*
>
> —Ruth Shaw Ernest

Giving Birds a Home

*B*irds really do like birdhouses, as long as you make them hospitable. Make a birdhouse fit into its surroundings both in color and texture as much as possible (twigs, bark, and unpainted materials are best; birds don't want to feel on display.) Place any house at least six feet off the ground and away from foot and cat traffic. Face it away from the sun, preferably in trees or shrubs. Don't despair if a bird doesn't move in till the second year the house is there; they need time to get used to it.

One easy bird-friendly option is to buy a standard birdhouse at a store and hot glue straw or dried grasses to the roof, creating a natural thatched effect. For more elaborate handmade houses, consult The Bird Feeder Book by Thom Boswell (Lark Books) and The Bird House Book by Bruce Woods and David Schoonmaker (also Lark Books). Lark (800-284-3388) also has a number of birdhouse and birdfeeder kits for sale.

> *Birds are as important as plants in my garden.*
>
> —Anne Scott-James

Spade Work

I am not a patient person by a long shot. I move quickly through my day and my life, wiggle and sigh and roll my eyes when forced to stand in line, and expect instant change in those I love (including myself). Being exposed to Buddhist meditation has helped me slow down or, more accurately recognize the need to slow down and respect the process, not the destination. So recently I've been thinking a lot about dirt.

Dirt as in soil and the sound preparation a garden needs. In the spring it's all about spade work, studying what nutrients are needed now so that my plants will get the nourishment to really flourish. Last year, an experienced gardening friend, when confronted in the heat of summer with my drooping tomatoes, told me I needed to double dig the garden patch (go two pitchforks deep into the soil and add compost) because the clay in my dirt was choking my plants.

This spring, as I dig deeper and deeper—hardened clay is not easy to break up—I'm struck by how much work that never shows overtly goes into a succcessful garden. It will be months before I find out if my digging is worth it. Today I'm just digging, not looking for quick fix, adding what is needed. Ah, yes.

> *Good gardening is very simple, really. You just*
> *have to learn to think like a plant.*
>
> —Barbara Damrosch

Grow Your Own

*D*id you know that you can grow your own luffa sponges? They are actually gourds and are available through many garden catalogs. Plant now and you can harvest next fall, enough not only for your family, but to give as gifts. To use, let the gourd ripen on the vine (it turns from green to yellow as it ripens.) But don't let it get fully yellow—slightly green means it will be a more tender sponge. When it's time to harvest, cut off the vine, peel the skin like an orange, and let it dry for about 10 days. Then cut it open from the big end, remove the seeds by shaking and strip off any more skin. Rinse the inside fibers and then submerge the sponge in water for 12 hours. Peel off the outside layer if any remains, and dry in the shade. If the sponge is too hard, you can soften by boiling them in water for five minutes.

> *No occupation is so delightful to me as the*
> *culture of the earth... and no culture comparable*
> *to that of the garden.... But though an old man,*
> *I am but a young gardener.*
>
> —Thomas Jefferson

Mowing Meditation

Nourshing Body
& Soul

My San Francisco friends think I'm crazy when I reveal that the highlight of visiting my mother's house in Alabama is mowing the yard. She has an expanse of grass that covers about two acres and an old riding lawn mower. I love to gas it up and engage in the routine of clutch cajoling and gas-pedal pushing until the relic feels like starting. I have a system. I start with the large perimeter and make the ensuing smaller circular rounds in each section until I hit the ultimate—that last small oval of grass that I can ride over in one final, graceful swoop. The hum of the motor, the patterns in the grass, the jolting of the rickety seat, the sweet smell—all give me an incredible sense of well-being coupled with a deep sense of gratitude for the moment.

> *The best place to find God is in a garden.*
>
> —George Bernard Shaw

Spring Cleaning

You can give your skin a great spring cleaning with all-natural products.

For oily skin:

Mix 1 egg white and 1 tablespoon of oatmeal. Apply in a thin layer to face and neck and leave for 15 to 20 minutes. Egg white contains papain, a natural enzyme that eliminates subcutaneous dirt and oil; the oatmeal is rich in protein and potassium and will give your skin a vital mineral boost.

For dry skin:

Spread a thin, even layer of honey on face and neck, taking care to avoid eyes. Honey is a natural humectant and traps moisture in the skin.

Homemade Alpha-Hydroxy Mask

Cook half of a diced and peeled apple in ¼ cup of milk until soft and tender. Mash, then cool to room temperature, and apply to skin. Thoroughly cleanse with warm water after 15–20 minutes.

> *I have always loved willows; they are the only trees who have wantonly escaped from the classic idea of a tree.*
>
> —Katharine Butler Hathaway

Garden Surprises

Every spring I make a trip to the nursery to load up on puny little plants that have no blooms. It's an act of faith, because half the time I have no idea what they'll look like. Then in summer, the color combinations in my garden come as a

Nourshing Body & Soul

wonderful surprise, far better than if I'd planned them. Gardening in spring is life affirming. The outcome is often less important than the promise of things to be, and the plants transforming in my flower beds remind me of the potential for growth in other areas of my life.

Good for What Ails You

If you suffer from menstrual cramps or premenstrual discomfort, you may find the following bath remedy to be soothing and calming. The water will dilate your blood vessels and relax your muscles, while the herbs provide aromatherapy.

> 2 tablespoons dried lavender
>
> 2 tablespoons dried rose petals
>
> 3 tablespoons dried chamomile
>
> 2 tablespoons hops

Combine the herbs in a glass or ceramic bowl and pour in a quart of boiling water. Cover and let sit for an hour. Strain the herbs and pour under the running tap of a warm (not hot) bath.

Weeding Vacation

*I*t was April and I was just plain exhausted from the effort of keeping my business afloat. I couldn't afford to go anywhere, so I decided to take a week off and do nothing. I slept, read, watched videos. But after a few days, I got a bit bored and so my husband and I decided to tackle the front yard, which had been ignored since we moved in the previous summer. The dry creek made of stones that dissected the property was overgrown with strawberry-like plants that yielded no edible fruit and seemed to smother everything else in sight. The previous owners knew nothing about plants and they had put shade-loving ones in full sun and sun-lovers in deep shade. Things were too close together; an ugly boxwood hedge rimmed the entire perimeter. . . It needed work.

My husband tackled the bigger project—moving various plants around—and I set to weeding the dry creek. Maybe it was because, like most of us in the modern world, I work in the intangible world of ideas all year, but as I sat there weeding patch after patch, exposing the stones as I worked, I felt an inordinate sense of satisfaction. It was so concrete: you pulled a weed, and then another and pretty soon a whole area was pristine and perfect. If only the world of business could be as tidy. Granted, later you'd have to do it all again, but at least you could see immediately the effects of your labor in stark brown earth. I enjoyed it so much that now I purposely take weeding vacations.

Nourshing Body
& Soul

A Good Workout

*G*ardening is good exercise. If you rake, hoe, dig, or pull weeds by hand, you can burn up to 300 calories per hour. The American Council on Exercise recommends that you do a brisk ten-minute walk before you start to warm up your body. Those with back problems (the most common gardening complaint) should take particular care to walk first. Back-sufferers should also be careful about lifting—bend those knees! And you might want to consider a knee pad for hand weeding.

Bathing in Mint

*B*e careful when you plant mint. Be sure you like it, and be sure you like it everywhere! I have seen people try a variety of ways to contain its virulent spread throughout the garden but the most ingenious was a woman who planted it in an old claw-foot bathtub. Her one word of caution—be sure to close the drain.

Besides peppermint, there is applemint (also known as wooly mint), black peppermint, orange mint, pineapple mint, and spearmint. Each has its own distinct flavor; all have many different uses. When harvesting mint for cooking, use only the top three to five leaves of each branch; the lower leaves are too pungent. Here are a few ways to try minting up your life.

Mint Foot Scrub

> 1 cup unflavored yogurt
>
> 1 cup kosher or rock salt
>
> ¾ cup mint leaves

Combine ingredients and apply to feet. Use a damp washcloth to gently scrub rough spots. Rinse feet and apply a thick lotion or petroleum jelly.

Natural Breath Freshener

Pass around a bowl of mint sprigs after dinner to deal with bad breath caused by garlic or onions.

Minty Facial Astringent

> 1 tablespoon fresh peppermint or spearmint
>
> 1 cup witch hazel

Combine ingredients in a jar with a tight-fitting lid. Steep in cool, dry place for one week, shaking occasionally. Strain and pour liquid into a bottle or spritzer. Use about 1 teaspoon per day. Good for normal and oily skin. Makes about a six-week supply.

Nourishing Body & Soul

May, Home

As I live with cancer, my healing lessons seem to be coming now from the garden. No small surprise since it is the place where I find culture and nature meeting. I love this land by the lake fiercely. I am forced to find sanity in the earth. Whenever I get back from traveling, I drop my suitcases at the door, strip off my shoes, and go directly to the dirt.

Yesterday I spent almost two hours being instructed by a huge Siberian iris plant that didn't bloom last year. I guessed it should be divided—a task I'd never attempted before. Indeed, as I dug in with a pitchfork, I saw that the roots were so entangled, so thickly enmeshed, I had to use a hack-saw to even begin to separate them all. It felt exactly like my mind, like my life. The iris plant has survived fire engines, two dogs' digging, and extreme frost. But what it told me is that its roots got so enmeshed because it didn't have the space it needed to go as deeply as is necessary to bloom. It will take me days to separate all of this complexity and then to build a new raised bed with very deep soil where each shoot can have the room it needs to root deeply enough so it can blossom.

That feels exactly what I need to do with my life as well.

Life begins the day you start a garden.

—Chinese proverb

Summer

What wondrous life is this I lead!
Ripe apples drop about my head;
The luscious clusters of the vine
Upon my mouth do crush their wine;
The nectarine and curious peach
Into my hands themselves do reach;
Stumbling on melons, as I pass,
Ensnared with flowers, I fall on grass.

—Andrew Marvell

In the Garden

Summer afternoon—summer afternoon; to me those have always been the two most beautiful words in the English language.

—Edith Wharton

Four-O'Clocks

S ome flowers are pure magic. I first learned that when I got a packet of flower seeds for a 4-H project one spring. The flowers were called four-o'clocks and, as evidenced by the brightly colored picture on the front, were quite showy. I eagerly dug up a bed in front of my house and sowed the seeds in wobbly rows. Every day, I ran out to check on the progress, which, of course, because I was an impatient eight-year-old, wasn't quick enough for me.

Finally, after an agonizing couple of weeks, the seedlings came poking through. They grew pretty rapidly—those that could survive my overwatering. I must confess that I had gotten bored with the plain green seedlings; then the first flower buds appeared. They all burst into bloom on practically the same day, filling the front of my house with a riot of color. I, too, was

In the Garden

bursting with pride and made all my family and neighbors look at the amazing miracle the seed packet had produced. By the time I had rounded everybody up, however, the flowers were closed up tightly. Every one of them! "That's why they're called four o'clocks," my mother explained. "Every day they close up at four o'clock sharp and open up with the fist rays of sun in the morning."

I checked every day and she was right. Four o'clock sharp. You could set your watch by my flowers!

Never give up listening to the sounds of birds.

—John James Audubon

Early Morning Garden

*T*he sun is almost up; the dogs give me soft leg nibbles, meaning, "Hungry! Hungry!" As I stand at the kitchen sink mixing three bowls of dog breakfast, I can watch the old California thrasher who's nesting in the neighbors' Mermaid Rose hedge, methodically plowing neat furrows in the damp leaf mold between our court bricks.

He lifts that big sickle bill, tilts his head to glance at the long window feeder. Any chance the titmice have left a few uncracked sunflower seeds? The broad wings spread as he flies to fly up to check—I can see the faint striping on his throat—lots of empty shells up there and one lone seed. Hammer, hammer with his powerful bill cracks the shell, then off to the babies in the nest in the rose hedge, big bill bulging breakfast.

From the creek comes the soft repeated question, "What?...What?" like drops of water splashing into a pool. "What!...What!" then the spiraling song of the Swanson's thrush, just arrived from Costa Rica. Early in the morning and again as evening falls, he'll be singing his sweet ascending song to us all summer. It's the dinner music for the barbecue, the symphony for the garden cocktail hour.

"Zig-a-zig-a-zig," from the very top of the dawn redwood comes the buzzing song of the male Anna's Hummingbird. His beautiful, bright gorget flashes rubies as he swings his small head back and forth in the first rays of the sun. Three dogs are breakfasting now as I step out to watch the diminutive songster. With a loud zip, he's off to the red bottle brush for sips of sweet nectar. He eats breakfast all morning; it takes a lot of fuel to keep that small engine running.

Early morning in the garden.

In the Garden

> *Flowers are sunshine, food, and medicine to*
> *the soul.*
>
> —Luther Burbank

Blown-In Pleasure

*T*his year my greatest garden delight comes from my magic planter that I bought for one dollar at an estate sale this spring. The owner had planted plastic flowers in it. I removed them and planted geishas, which promptly died. I decided that was a sign and gave up. Then, mid-summer I happened to look over at it and it was covered with daisies in full bloom. A complete gift that had blown in from some other yard!

All is miracle. The stupendous order of nature, the revolution of a hundred millions of worlds around a million of suns, the activity of light, the life of animals, all are grand and perpetual miracles.

—Voltaire

Old Roses

*P*erhaps because of the advantage of coming from a family of flower lovers, I am a bit of a snob about roses. For me, they have to be old, old, old, or I turn up my nose. You can tell the difference between old roses and the new fancy hybrid kinds so easily—the distinctive scents, the big falling-apart, loose petals. Old roses are like the women who grew them originally, like my aunts—very dignified, wearing simple and subtle colors, and with a scent of purest essence of rose. New roses are exotic and pretty to look at, but it is the old roses that have rooted in my memory and stay forever.

Finding Old Roses

O ld roses are not only beautiful, but they have the advantage of being more disease resistant and drought tolerant than the finicky hybrid tea roses. Two good suppliers of old roses are Roayll River Roses (800-820-5830, $3 for catalog) and the Antique Rose Emporium (800-441-0002, $4). Both offer the history on the origins of many old fashioned roses.

> *If I give you a rose, you will not doubt of God.*
>
> —Clement of Alexander

The Shape of Things

A t times, it seems to me quite an obvious sort of pleasure. Yet I still find the shapes and colors of flowers to be truly amazing. Last year I decided to plant some flowers to attract butterflies and hummingbirds. One was a cleome, which I had

In the Garden

never tried before. Unfortunately I planted it in the early fall, just after the heat of the summer, hoping to have flowers fairly quickly. (I am still new to the art of gardening and have not learned to trust that other people know a lot more than I do. This is a double-edged sword. On the one hand, I tend to begin things in the wrong season with little success even though someone has told me it won't work. On the other, I find I can grow some wonderful plants that catalogs and books say are not possible in my area. So, I keep experimenting.)

Well, four cleomes sprouted and began to grow. I was very optimistic and was looking forward to their flowering by Thanksgiving. I waited and waited and waited. The plants grew to about a foot tall by Christmas and then decided to lay low for the rest of the winter. Discouraged, I wondered if any bloom would ever show up. After the last frost, I transplanted them into a space in the garden and waited again.

Finally they grew a bit more but it wasn't until June that the growth really took off. Then within a month I had buds and my first flowers. What incredible flowers. Solid, pure tones of pink or white with a shape that seems to be from science fiction: Four oval petals in a vertical fan shape with the pistil and five or six stamen coming way out from the center of the flower like martian antennae. Truly an out-of-this world beauty, worth all the wait.

My love of shapes and colors can drive my wife a little crazy (she believes in wide swatches of color and shapes that look good from a distance, whereas I tend to focus on the look of the individual flower and ignore the whole), so I have a small part of the yard to do anything I wish. It often looks jumbled and the colors never tend to match, but every time I go there and look at each flower and take in its wonderful colors and shape, I am in awe.

> Nothing is more completely the child of art than a garden.
>
> —Sir Walter Scott

Scarecrow Help

*I*f you're plagued by birds and aren't up to making your own straw-filled scarecrow, you can buy a frame from The Natural Gardening Company that can be dressed in your rag-bag clothes (707-766-9303).

In the Garden

> Summer to me would be incomplete without the dandelions. For what they symbol, would that there were more in the drifted dust of the cities.
>
> —Henry Williamson

True Confessions

I have a confession to make that I hope my father never hears—I love weeding. During the summers when I was small, my father used to pay me fifty cents an hour to pull weeds from our extensive gardens. I suppose, looking back on my wage scale, it was a great deal for him, but it was even better for me. It was such a feeling of accomplishment to finish a square area and look down at all that sweet-smelling, moist dirt and not see a single little invader.

Blessed with more garden space than one boy could keep weed free, it seemed at the time a source of unlimited riches—all for doing what was fun in the first place. One particularly ambitious summer, I would set my alarm clock for sunrise in order to give myself time to weed away the morning hours and still leave plenty of time for more normal summer activities. At the tender age of ten, I planted a vegetable garden that covered nearly a quarter acre of land and worked diligently every day, weeding and playing Panama Canal with my extensive series of irrigation ditches.

All that training has conditioned me so strongly that now all I need to do to return to childlike peace is to plant myself in the garden. It must sound truly corny, but what a great way to get grounded—on your hands and knees in the dirt, face down, all attention focused on seeking out those unwanted little weeds.

Without the blackbird, in whose throat the
sweetness of the green fields dwells, the days
would be only partly summer.

—Richard Jefferies

Lazy Summer Days

I can't possibly count the hundreds of summer hours I used to spend in the fields around my parents' house, lying in the tall grass, the hot sun beating down, the smell of green strong in the air. I was mostly alone, searching for butterflies and dragonflies, making daisy and clover chains, just whiling away the hours. With a friend, we'd pick buttercups and hold them under one another's chins to see if we liked butter and pull petals off daisies to find out who the boy down the street favored: "He loves me, he loves me not." It was forty years ago, but the rush of memories come flooding back. And I mourn for the lost fields, all covered in houses now, and the lost freedom of children, who must be supervised and shepherded wherever they go.

Ah, summer, what power you have to make us
suffer and like it.

—Russell Baker

In the Garden

The Satisfactions of Herbs

On a warm summer's day, the delightful scents of rosemary, mint, and lavender perfume the air as bees and hummingbirds go about their feeding. Perhaps you harvest a handful of lavender to scent your underwear drawer. Later you run out to snip some parsley and chives to add zest to a salad and throw together a bouquet of bright-red bergamot and silvery artemisia for the dinner table. Or maybe today is the day you create fragrant potpourri and dried wreaths from the bounty of your garden to please the eyes and noses of friends and family.

Nothing is more pleasing, useful, and easy than growing an herb garden, even if you only have a tiny plot of land. You don't even really need a yard, because herbs can be easily grown in pots on a deck or terrace or even indoors if you have a sunny window. If you do have outdoor space, tuck them in the border of a flower garden or in a patch in the vegetable garden or simply plant them directly outside the kitchen door, like they do in France, so you simply lean outside when you want something. Because they are virtually indestructible, they are perfect for beginning gardeners. Most are fast growing and pest resistant. Chances are your only problem may be how quickly they spread; some can be quite invasive.

Choosing what to grow is a pleasure in and of itself. Think about what and how you cook and whether you would like to make your own flower crafts and potpourris. Then pick accordingly. I personally hate to pay for a bunch of dill at the store because when I need it, I want only a little, and the rest always spoils in the fridge. So dill was at the top of my list. Some other common culinary herbs to consider: basil, chives, marjoram, mint, oregano, parsley, rosemary, sage, savory, and thyme. If you want a scented garden and plan to make bouquets, potpourris, wreaths, etc., you might want to plant bergamot (beautiful shaggy red flowers), dyer's chamomile, lady's mantle, lamb's ears, lavender, lemon balm, lemon verbena, nasturtiums, rue, santolina, tansy, violets, woodruff, and yarrow.

Here are the sweet peas, on tiptoe for a flight . . .

—John Keats

Ode To Morning Glories

I have realized anew the almost spiritual beauty of the common morning glory. I avoided planting these flowers anywhere about the garden, because they seed so freely that they soon become an annoyance, strangling more important plants and even tangling up the vegetables mischievously. Instead, I have given them a screen that breaks the bareness of the tool house, and let them run riot. The leaves are not especially notable, being rather coarse, but the flowers are as exquisite in

In the Garden

their richly colored fragility as if Aurora, in the bath, had amused herself by blowing bubbles. These, catching the sunrise glow, floated away upon the breeze and, falling on a wayside vine, opened into flowers that from their origin vanish again under the sun's caress.

Among all their colors none is more beautiful or unusual than the rich purple with the ruddy throat merging to white—night shadows melting into the clear of dawn.

> *The earth laughs in flowers.*
>
> —Ralph Waldo Emerson

Beautiful Weeds

*I*t's amazing how the variety of flowers and their availability changes throughout the United States. In the south I was used to a profusion of wild flowers—black-eyed susans, sweet peas, Queen Anne's lace, daylilies—lining the roads and filling the fields. I picked freely without consequence or expense and our house never lacked a bouquet or two. I've never quite grown accustomed to life in San Francisco where I have to actually pay for these same flowers at a florist or farmer's market. My mother laughed at me for buying Queen Anne's lace for my wedding bouquet; "Why do you want a weed in there?" she asked. And I realized that through sheer geography, Queen Anne's lace has become a unique and beautiful flower to me that is worth every penny.

> *June reared that bunch of flowers you carry,*
> *From seeds of April's sowing.*
>
> —Robert Browning

Confessions of a Tomato Grower

Some of my most sublime moments have been at four in the morning when the irrigation water comes through. Alone, under a full moon, in the garden, you see subtle variations. Sometimes I look at the foliage of my tomatoes and think I would grow tomatoes even if they didn't grow fruit. It's like looking at the stars as your eyes become accustomed to the dark. First you see a thousand stars, then you see ten thousand.

> *The cherry tomato is a wonderful invention,*
> *producing, as it does, a satisfactorily explosive*
> *squish when bitten.*
>
> —Miss Manners

In the Garden

Detoxify Your Garden

You don't need a mass of chemical pesticides, weed killers, and fertilizers to have a lush garden. There are a number of things you can do to reduce the amount of chemicals on your fruit, vegetables, and flowers, which in turn will reduce the amount of such items in the water and air and limit exposure to birds, bees, butterflies, your children, and yourself. First, start a compost pile (see directions on page 155); it should eliminate your need for nonorganic fertilizer. Ask your nursery about organic ways of fertilizing lawns; there are several. Learn about biological ways of controlling pests: praying mantises, spiders, and ladybugs reduce harmful insects. My only method of aphid control for two dozen rose bushes is to buy a batch of ladybugs at the beginning of the flowering season; it works like a charm. Ladybugs are available at most nurseries and through catalogs such as Plow & Hearth (which also has great things like butterfly sanctuaries and nesting birdhouses for sale; call 800-627-1712 for a catalog).

You can also plant flowers that attract beneficial insects. Good ones include all the daisies, plants in the carrot family (Queen Anne's lace, sweet alyssum, chervil, and caraway) and anything in the mint family, including basil and oregano (yup, they're mints too). And when choosing plants in the first place, consider how disease and insect resistant they are; for example,

Tropicana roses attract more aphids than Angel Face.

There are all kinds of bug deterring herbs that can be planted as companions to various vegetables and flowers: Marigolds are the workhorse here; they deter most bugs. Garlic should be planted between rose bushes to keep away Japanese beetles. Basil repels flies and mosquitoes and helps tomatoes grow. Horseradish helps keep potato bugs away. Mint and peppermint deter white cabbage moths. Ask at your nursery for a complete list.

Decide how much damage you can live with and go for the lowest impact strategy—sometimes a strong blast with the garden hose will work wonders. Hot chilies are an effective insecticide. Chop up a few hot ones and mix with detergent and water and spray on plants (you can add garlic and onion too for a real kick). Or dust plants with ground chili pepper. There are also a number of very effective, yet harmless herbal pesticides including Ryania (used against aphids and Japanese beetles and certain moths), white hellebore (good against slugs, caterpillars, and other leaf-munching pests), pyrethrum (effective against slugs) nicotine and derris (good for controlling aphids, caterpillars), and rotenone (good general insecticide, effective also against fleas on pets).

If you must use chemicals, read the labels. Those labeled "Danger-Poison" should not be used by backyard gardeners. Those labeled "Caution" are the least dangerous and therefore less harmful. Soaps and oils are lower in toxicity than sprays

In the Garden

and powders, and spot treatment is less harmful than broad-spectrum spraying. Never apply chemicals in the heat of the day or in the presence of children or pets, and make sure the garden has completely dried before letting kids or pets back outside. Store such items out of the reach of kids. To receive the Environmental Protection Agency's free pamphlets on the subject, call (800-490-9198).

> *When you can put your foot on seven daisies*
> *summer is come.*
>
> —Proverb

Bug-Eating Birds

Another way to eliminate the need for pesticides is to encourage our feathered friends to dine at your house. Here's how: (1) Place birdbaths throughout the garden, away from bushes that can hide cats. Keep them clean and filled with fresh water; (2) Create a fountain with trickling water; the sound and movement is attractive to birds; (3) Plant a diverse array of plants, particularly natives; (4) Don't use any chemicals on your garden as they can kill birds. For answers to all kinds of bird questions, you can call Cornell University's Laboratory of Ornithology (607-254-2473) or the National Audubon Society's

Bird and Wildlife Information Center (212-979-3080; website www.audubon.org).

Being Prepared

I always keep a bucket filled with whatever tools I may need in my garden. I started this after years of saying, "Oh that rose needs pruning; I'll go get my clippers" or "That tomato needs staking; I'll do it tomorrow." Needless to say the roses didn't get pruned nor the tomatoes staked. Now I always take my bucket, which has my clippers, scissors, hand rake, stakes, and twine in it. I'm prepared to take care of most garden woes on the spot, and my garden looks better as a consequence.

> *Summer is a promissory note signed in June, its long days spent and gone before you know it, and due to be repaid next January.*
>
> —Hal Borland

Lovely Lobelia

In the Garden

F or years I lived in a house on a steep hill that had no yard for gardening. But each year I would plant a variety of lobelia in a strawberry pot on my tiny landing. By summer the pot would be covered in tiny, cascading blossoms—a meditation on the color blue: deep, almost midnight blue with a white center; solid royal blue the palest baby blue, and bright violet blue. As evening fell, I would take my chair outside and watch the colors glow in the fading light.

Sometimes in June, when I see unearned
dividends of dew hung on every lupine, I have
doubts about the real poverty of the sands.

—Aldo Leopold

Ghost Garden

Where I come from, there are many ramshackle houses. In shades of ghostly grey, their inhabitants have grown up and moved out, leaving the sad, spectral houses behind. The luckier of these houses, along the banks of the Ohio River, get reclaimed and become showplaces, at least one of which has graced the pages of *Architectural Digest*. Mostly though, they wait. While the houses sag and creak, the gardens go wild! Plantings and hedges, once neat and tidy, are out of control, buzzing with birds, bees, and heaven knows what. Every spring and summer as a child, I would pick flowers in these abandoned yards and set up a table at the bottom of my driveway to sell bouquets in old coffee cans to passing neighbors.

One such house I know burned to the ground during the night, leaving a charred and barren lot where once had been some river captain's pride. I was sad because the hydrangeas were gone, and I had my eye on them, both for bouquets and for transplanting in my mother's garden. The next year, an amazing thing happened around the outer perimeters of the burned-down old manse: A "ghost garden" was growing in exactly the same formation! Bulbs, hedges, and even the hydrangeas all came back at an astonishing pace. And thanks to all the rusting copper pipes, hinges, and nails scattered half-buried in the soil after the fire, the hydrangeas, a pristine white the year before, were the bluest of blues. I decided not to take any. Those hydrangeas had been so loyal to that yard, they simply could not move anywhere else.

> *Won't you come into my garden? I would like my roses to see you.*
>
> —Richard Sheridan

In the Garden

With Family and Friends

*Flowers leave some of their fragrance in the hand
that bestows them.*

—Chinese proverb

Fairy Bouquets

My dad was a great gardener, and when I was a little girl, he used to take me out early in the summer morning before my mother woke up to make fairy bouquets. We would pick only the tiniest flowers—violets, miniature roses, baby nasturtiums—place them into tiny bud vases or old spice jars, sometimes adding a bit of ribbon around the neck of the container, and put them at our breakfast plate. I loved doing it and it was so fun to see my mother's face when she came down to eat!

> *Oh, this is the joy of the rose:*
> *That it blows,*
> *And goes.*

—Willa Cather

*With Family
& Friends*

Moon River Vines

Growing up in the south, my summers were filled with shade trees, brazenly colored flowers, and choking vegetation in the form of wild morning glories and patches of kudzu that resembled small green seas. With so much growing and tangling about you, it's easy to understand why my family and I love gardening so much. My Uncle Robert loved vines and cultivated, cataloged, and saved seeds, which he doled out to the rest of us. His prize was the moon river vine whose rather ordinary looking seeds held within their brown casing nothing short of a miracle to my cousins and me. Early each summer, Uncle Robert would take the seeds out of an old pill bottle and give us each 3–5 of them with instructions to plant them near a trellis or porch column and keep them watered. Within six weeks, there would be a delicate vine with papery thin leaves that grew at an astonishing rate. By mid-July the buds would appear, luminous white, like twisted-up tissue paper.

From then on, every summer night at dusk we'd gather on the porch with our ice tea and try to act blasé as we furtively glanced every few minutes at the buds of the vine. Our childish patience would eventually be rewarded with a small sway from the vine, sometimes a tiny twitch, then ever so slowly a bud would begin to open before our very eyes, eventually, over the course of about half an hour, unfurling into a saucer-sized pure white flower. The smell was heavenly—rivaling that of magnolias and jasmine—but fainter and more elusive. We were never allowed to touch the flowers or—God forbid—pick them, and I honestly don't think I ever wanted to. I was awestruck by their amazing aliveness. Sometimes we'd turn off the porch light and get to stay up a little later than usual to see if a lunar moth would visit the irresistible flowers; sometimes even a tiny bat would appear. Beyond the porch the lightning bugs would signal to one another, and a symphony of night sounds serenaded us. It was magic.

> *Fame is the scentless sunflower, with a gaudy*
> *crown of gold;*
>
> *But friendship is the breathing rose, with sweets*
> *in every fold.*
>
> —Oliver Wendell Holmes

Personalized Pumpkins

If you grow pumpkins, you can scratch names, dates, phrases, hearts, etc., into them with an ice pick or other sharp implement as they begin to grow. The scratch will heal over, and as the pumpkin gets bigger, so does your message. (Just think of the possibilities—kids especially enjoy such a surprise).

With Family
& Friends

Dragon-Lady Dahlias

My Aunt Myrtle had a small house where she cultivated one of the most envied gardens in northern Alabama. Her lawn was quilted with daffodils and tulips in the spring, and in summer she grew legions of leggy sunflowers and brilliant cannas. My favorites were her dahlias. They grew taller than me, and some of the flowers were bigger than my head. She would pick me a bouquet and we'd pretend they were elegant, feathery hats as I held them behind my ears. They came in all shades from lipstick pink to bright yellow, but there was one shade of red so intense it seemed to smolder. My aunt called these her dragon-lady dahlias. For me they conjured up fantasy meetings with beautiful women dressed in exotic silk gowns with beaded headdresses and long, tiny nails with crimson polish. They were intoxicating to look at, and I could spend hours engaged in my own little dramas amid their searing faces. I buy dahlia bouquets every chance I get but have yet to find any as alluring as Aunt Myrtle's dragon ladies.

Homegrown Is Best

Quite often, almost as an afterthought as I am on my way out the door, I bring a small bouquet of seasonal flowers to a friend . What is in season is humble and hardly comparable to the thing a florist would deliver to your door. But the fragrance of fresh cut sweet peas or the unexpected loveliness of onion tops and heliotrope mixed in with a few puny dahlias and zinnias make for a delightful surprise gift that is as wonderful to give as it is to receive.

> *And what is so rare as a day in June?*
> *Then, if ever, come perfect days;*
> *Then Heaven tries the earth if it be in tune,*
> *And over it softly her warm ear lays.*
>
> —James Russell Lowell

Speak the Language of Flowers

We all know roses mean "I love you," but do you know the nonverbal messages of other flowers? The Victorians used to practice the "language of flowers," in which they would send little nosegays of homegrown flowers that were actually nonverbal poems. A bouquet of coreopsis and ivy, for example, would mean, "always cheerful friendship." Such floral messages are called tussie-mussies, a term that dates back to the 1400s when these nosegays first came into fashion; they were routinely carried by both men and women.

With Family
& Friends

The language of flowers was quite complex. If, for example, the flowers were presented upside down, the message was the opposite—a upside down rose, for example, meant "I don't love you." If the bow or the flower bent to the left, the message referred to the receiver "you have beautiful eyes". If it bends to the right, the message refers to the sender. "I send loving thoughts" says the left-leaning pansy. If you added leaves to your tussy-mussy, they signaled hope, while thorns meant danger. When you received a tussy-mussy, touching it to your lips meant you agreed with the message's sentiments. If you tore off the petals and threw them down, you were sending a strong rejection of the sentiment.

Tussie-mussies are easy to make. Simply decide on your message and pick the appropriate flowers, leaving six inches of stem. Strip stems of leaves, and pick the largest flower for the center. Wrap its stem with floral tape. Then add the remaining flowers in a circle, taping the stems together as you go, keeping the height even, until you reach a diameter of about 5 inches. Then add greens, if any. Finish off by winding tape down the length of the stems, and add a ribbon streamer or a piece of lace as a bow. Voila! Send with a card explaining the flowers' meanings. Tussey-mussies should be kept in water.

Say it with Flowers

Apple blossom: Preference

Azalea: First love

Coreopsis: Always cheerful

Cornflowers: Healing, felicity

Daffodil: Regard

Red Dianthus: Lively and pure affection

Heliotrope: Accommodating disposition

Ivy: Friendship

Johnny Jump-up: Happy thoughts

Lamb's Ear: Gentleness

Lavender: Devotion

Lily of the Valley: Return of happiness

Love-in-a-mist: Kiss me twice before I rise

Mint: Warmth of feeling

Oregano: Joy

Pansy: Loving thoughts

Red Salvia: Energy and esteem

Rosemary: Devotion

Scented geranium: Preference

Thyme: Courage and strength

Violets: Faithfulness

Wallflower: Fidelity in adversity

*With Family
& Friends*

White Clover: Good luck

Yarrow: Health

Zinnia: Thought of absent friends

A Tiara of Fireflies

Our grandma always wore hair nets to keep her silver hair in place. As the nets wore out or snagged, Gram would give them to us girls. On special evenings my sis and I would weave garlands of daisies and wildflowers and pin them in our hair. Our brother would bring in a canning jar full of fireflies, and we would tip it into Gram's hair nets, loosely fit them over our fancy hairdos, and have twinkling tiaras for an evening of garden play.

The sound of birds stops the noise in my mind.

—Carly Simon

Meagan's Garden

When my four-year-old granddaughter arrived for a week-long visit in early summer, I was determined to introduce her to the joys of gardening. I told her we'd make a garden just for her. We found a patch of yard and prepared the soil.

Then we headed for the garden center, where she wanted one of every seedling she saw. Eventually we ended up with a reasonable number of flowers that would do well and promptly planted them. She then made a sign saying "Meagan's Garden" which we planted in the center. After she left, I sent her photos all summer so she could see how her garden was doing. And she returned with her whole family for Labor Day and proudly showed off her patch to her parents.

Sustaining Delights

*M*y favorite garden memories are from the vegetable gardens my grandfather grew during the depression when I was a little girl. My father was a high school teacher long before unions and pay raises, and my grandparents had lost all their savings when the banks folded.

We spent all summer with my grandparents in Maine. My grandfather planted a garden large enough to feed all six of us and supply my mother and grandmother with produce to can for the winter. The garden was beautifully kept with the lowest vegetables in the front—carrots, radishes, beets, parsnips. Then three kinds of beans—green and shell (too cold for limas in Maine). Then polebeans, corn, and popcorn. Off to the side was a rambling mass of cucumbers and squash. Pumpkins

With Family & Friends

were planted in between the last two rows of corn.

Everyday the noon meal consisted of any and all vegetables that were ready. And I always rode home at the end of the summer in the backseat of the car squeezed in between boxes of full canning jars.

Homegoing

I remember the back yard and July and home and being fifteen and digging in black dirt, a yardful of gardens and weeds between me and the house, when milkweed down floated up, like a kiss of magic on a calm wind. From the balcony, my parents were calling me.

The breath of that moment stays with me, and now, from the city, I sometimes drift home across the miles to where I heard God in the wind and whispering leaves; my hands caked in dirt and head full of magic and milkweed down. I ride on updrafts, swallowing miles in between.

But my family counts the miles in-between; thinking miles and counting miles are unimportant to me. They don't see me on the milkweed down, floating to them, swollen with laughter and home, or tumbling breathless into the surrounding dirt where daylilies nod appreciative heads in the wind.

I don't know the future or where this wind will carry me

next year. So here I thrust my hands in the dirt of a new place that nourishes me. Here I've decided to make my new home, and I look at my new garden and call down to the dahlias, telling them of an enchanted home where distance was only the space in-between the horizon and house and not you and me. Where leaves whispered and God was in the dirt.

My fingers were my roots that grew in that dirt when I weeded and plunged my hands down and knew the garden was bigger than me. The words the dahlias sigh back are a secret the garden will keep just between us. It's about summer and home and hot July wind that plants milkweed down softly in the dirt far away from home. My family still calls me from endless in-betweens.

> *It is forbidden to live in a town which has no greenery.*
>
> —The Jerusalem Talm

With Family
& Friends

Into the Kitchen

*The smell of manure, of sun on foliage, of evapo-
rating water, rose to my head; two steps farther
and I could look down into the vegetable garden
enclosed within its tall pale fence of reeds—rich
chocolate earth studded emerald green, frothed
with the white of cauliflowers, jewelled with the
purple globes of eggplant and the scarlet wealth
of tomatoes.*

—Doris Lessing

Summer's Healthful Harvest

We know gardening is good exercise, but research is now showing that eating the bounty from our gardens is also good for our health. Here's the lowdown on the most popular summer crops:

Tomatoes: One medium tomato has half the (RDA) recommended daily allowance of vitamin C and 20 percent of the RDA of fiber and vitamin A. It also contains lycopene, an antioxidant that appears to reduce the risk of heart attack and of various cancers, including breast and prostate.

Into the Kitchen

Corn: Excellent source of fiber and two antioxidants—lutein and zeaxanthin—that may lower the risk for macular degeneration, which is the leading cause of blindness in older folks.

Sweet Peppers: These are little powerhouses of vitamins A and C. Green peppers have twice as much vitamin C as oranges; yellow and red peppers have four times the C! They also are good sources of immune system enhancing B-6 and folic acid, which helps against heart disease and has been recently discovered to prevent neural tube defects in developing fetuses.

Zucchini: You may get sick of eating it, but this low-cal wonder is full of vitamins C and A and is also high in fiber, which helps prevent heart attacks and colon cancer.

The work of a garden bears visible fruits—in a world where most of our labours seem suspiciously meaningless.

—Pam Brown

The Problem of Plenty

No gardener worth his or her salt would be without a plethora of recipes to handle the abundance of green beans, corn, tomatoes, cucumbers, and, especially, zucchini that even a tiny garden can produce. Here a few particularly tasty ones.

Stuffed Garden

This is a traditional recipe in Spain. You can make it with all one vegetable, but then you'll have to call it something else.

2 large onions, peeled but left whole

2 large whole green peppers

2 medium zucchini

pinch of saffron

2 bay leaves

¼ teaspoon nutmeg

2 cloves

2 large fresh tomatoes

2 cloves garlic, peeled and chopped

14 ounce can chopped tomatoes

4 tablespoons olive oil

salt and pepper

4 ounces bacon, trimmed of fat

2 tablespoons lightly toasted pine nuts

3 tablespoons bread crumbs

1 cup cooked rice

4 tablespoons grated Parmesean cheese

2 tablespoons white wine or water

Into the Kitchen

Blanch the whole onions, peppers, and zucchini in a large pan of boiling water, removing peppers and zucchini after 5 minutes and onions after 15. Allow to cool. Pour off all but ½ cup of the water and add the saffron, bay leaves, nutmeg, and cloves and simmer for 10 minutes. Set spiced water aside.

Meanwhile, using a sharp knive and a spoon, cut the tops of the tomatoes and scoop out the insides, leaving a shell thick enough for stuffing. Chop the tomato insides. In a small saucepan, combine 1 tablespoon oil, the garlic, and all of the chopped tomato. Cook over medium heat for 10 minutes, until it becomes saucelike. Add salt and pepper and set aside

Preheat oven to 400° F. Using a spoon and a sharp knife, scoop out the center of the onions, leaving a thin outer shell. Chop the centers. Cut the zucchini in half and scoop out the center, again chopping the insides. Cut the tops off the peppers and remove seeds and membranes, keeping the peppers whole.

Heat the rest of the oil and the bacon, sauté chopped onions, and zucchini until onion is wilted and bacon is crispy.

In a large bowl, combine the bacon mixture with the pine nuts, 2 tablespoons of bread crumbs, half of the tomato sauce, salt and pepper, rice, and wine or water. Place the vegetable shells in a large baking pan and stuff with the stuffing mixture. Top with remaining tomato sauce, bread crumbs, and grated cheese. Carefully pour the spiced water into the pan so that vegetables are sitting in about ½ inch of water. Bake until vegetable shells are soft to touch and stuffing is heated through, about 35 minutes. Add more spiced water to keep from scorching if necessary. Serves 8 as a sidedish; 4 as a main course.

Green Bean, Corn, and Tomato Salad

> 1 pound green beans, cut into 1-inch lengths
>
> kernels from 3 ears of corn
>
> $\frac{1}{2}$ cup white wine vinegar
>
> 6 tablespoons olive oil
>
> 5 tablespoons sugar
>
> 3 large tomatoes, chopped
>
> $\frac{1}{2}$ cup chopped red onion
>
> $\frac{1}{3}$ cup chopped fresh parsley
>
> Salt and pepper to taste

Cook beans in large saucepan of boiling water for 2 minutes. Add corn kernels and cook until vegetables are crisp-tender, about 2 minutes longer. Drain well.

Whisk vinegar, oil, and sugar in large bowl to blend. Add beans, corn, tomatoes, onion, and parsley; toss to coat. Season with salt and pepper. Cover and chill at least 2 hours or overnight. Serves 6.

Into the Kitchen

Roasted Tomato and Red Pepper Soup

> $2\frac{1}{4}$ pounds tomatoes, halved lengthwise
>
> 2 large red bell peppers, seeded and quartered

1 onion, cut into thick slices

4 large garlic cloves, peeled

2 tablespoons olive oil

1 teaspoon fresh thyme leaves or $\frac{1}{2}$ teaspoon dried

water

Preheat oven to 450° degrees. Arrange tomatoes (cut side up), bell peppers, onion, and garlic cloves on a large baking sheet. Drizzle oil over; sprinkle generously with salt and pepper. Roast vegetables until brown and tender, turning peppers and onion occasionally, about 40 minutes. Remove from oven. Cool.

Transfer vegetables and any accumulated juices to food processor and add thyme. Puree soup, gradually adding about 2 cups of water to thin soup to desired consistency. Chill until cold, about 3 hours. (Can be prepared 1 day ahead. Cover and keep refrigerated. If soup becomes too thick, thin with water to desired consistency). Serves 4.

Vegetable Gratin

2 $\frac{1}{2}$ tablespoons butter

2 tablespoons olive oil

1 medium onion, chopped

2 garlic cloves, minced

1 medium-size green bell pepper, diced

8 smallish summer squashes (such as crookneck, pattypan, ronde de Nice, or zucchini), about 2 pounds total, cut into $\frac{1}{2}$-inch cubes

kernels from 2 ears of corn

Salt and pepper to taste

¼ cup flour

½ cup cornmeal

4 tablespoons fresh basil, or thyme, or a combination of both

2 eggs, beaten

1 cup low fat milk

3 tablespoons freshly grated Parmesan cheese

Preheat oven to 350°. Grease a shallow gratin dish or other baking dish with ½ tablespoon of the butter. Place 1 tablespoon butter and the olive oil in a skillet over medium heat. Add the onions, garlic, and green pepper; saute over medium-high heat for 5 minutes.

Add the squash, corn, and salt and pepper; saute another 4 to 5 minutes, until the squash is nearly tender. Remove from heat and set aside.

Mix together the flour, cornmeal, basil and/or thyme. Stir in the eggs, milk, and vegetables.

Spoon the mixture into the prepared dish and bake for 25 to 30 minutes or until a crust has formed and a knife inserted into the center comes out nearly clean. Dot with the remaining 1 tablespoon butter, sprinkle the cheese on top, and bake for 7 to 10 minutes longer, until the crust has browned slightly and the edges are bubbling and crispy. Serve hot or at room temperature. Serves 6.

Into the Kitchen

Caprese Salad

This only works with vine-ripened tomatoes; if all you have are the rubbery store-versions, wait until you can find some real tomatoes.

1 tablespoon fresh lemon juice

6 tablespoons olive oil

3 tablespoons red wine vinegar

4–5 tomatoes, cut into ½-inch slices

1 large red onion, julienned

8 ounces mozzarella, thinly sliced

15–20 fresh basil leaves

Combine lemon juice, olive oil, and vinegar in a jar or container with an airtight lid. Shake vigorously for a full minute. Chill.

On a large plate, layer onion slices, tomatoes, and mozzarella. Garnish liberally with fresh basil. Pour the dressing over the salad immediately before serving. Serves 6–8 as an appetizer.

Old-Fashioned Mustard Pickles

This recipe from my French grandmother is not for the faint of heart. It makes the puckeryist pickles I've ever tasted. Everyone in my family loves them—and I hope you will to. It makes a lot, but you can cut the recipe down proportionately.

4 dry quarts small pickling cucumbers, with stems (A dry quart is ¹⁄₆ more than a liquid quart, says *Joy of Cooking*)

¹⁄₂ gallon white vinegar

¹⁄₂ cup salt

¹⁄₂ cup dry mustard

1 teaspoon powdered alum

Wash cucumbers carefully. In a large crock, mix remaining ingredients and add cucumbers. (Add more vinegar if necessary to cover cucumbers completely in liquid). Cover and store in a cool, dark place for 3 weeks, stirring occasionally. When pickles are ready, refrigerate for longer life. Makes 1 crock. (If you have no crock, mix the ingredients in a large bowl, place pickles in jars, then pour vinegar mixture over. Store in cool dry place for 3 weeks, shaking jars occasionally).

Crisp Delight

One of my greatest garden pleasures is to receive compliments on the rhubarb-strawberry crisp I bake for almost every summer barbecue. Our rhubarb plant was well established in the garden when we moved into our house fifteen years ago. The plant is so prolific that I give away a fresh bunch to every rhubarb lover who enters the door. Though not all our guests favor this beautiful celerylike plant topped with magnificent poisonous leaves, when they see the crisp warm from the oven with its sugary top and juicy bottom, they cannot resist this old

Into the Kitchen

standby. Add ice cream and wait for the compliments to come pouring in.

Surefire Rhubarb Strawberry Crisp

   3 cups rhubarb, sliced

   2 cups strawberries, whole or sliced

   juice from one lemon

   1 stick butter, softened

   1 cup granulated sugar

   1 cup flour

Preheat oven to 400°. Combine rhubarb, strawberries, and lemon juice in a 9 x 13-inch baking pan. In a medium bowl, combine the butter, sugar, and flour until crumbly and then spread over rhubarb mixture. Bake uncovered for 20 minutes or until crisp is bubbly and top browned. Serves 6.

The best things that can come out of the garden
are gifts for other people.

—Jamie Jobb

The Fruits of Summer

I love summer fruit—especially plums, nectarines, and cherries. I think one of the reasons they taste so delicious is because their season is so short. I never quite manage to get my fill, and they're gone from the stores. Once I went cherry picking in upstate New York, and even with my "one for the bucket, one for my mouth" picking method, I never did reach the saturation point.

When I was a teenager, I taught swimming at an overnight camp on a lake in my hometown. Even though it was so close to home, I lived at camp, and while I greatly enjoyed that first taste of freedom, the food—instant mashed potatoes and powdered eggs—left much to be desired. So every few days, as I was standing on the docks supervising the swimmers, my father would drive up in his VW Bug and hand a paper sack out the window. My fresh fruit supply.

Stuffed Baked Peaches

10 fresh peaches, pitted and halved

1 egg yolk

7 tablespoons butter, softened

1 cup of crushed Amaretto di Saronni cookies

Remove one spoonful of peach flesh from each peach and puree; set aside. Cream 6 tablespoons of butter in a bowl, stirring in egg yolk, peach puree, and crushed cookies until well combined. Fill each peach half with a generously rounded scoop of the mixture.

Into the Kitchen

Place the peach halves, open side up, in a large glass casserole with the remaining tablespoon of butter, and bake in a preheated oven at 375° for 5–7 minutes or until cookie mixture is lightly browned. Serve peaches at room temperature with crème fraîche or ice cream. Serves 10.

Peach or Nectarine Clafouti

This is a marvelous low-fat dessert that's perfect for late summer when peaches and nectarines are abundant.

1¼ cups low-fat milk

¼ cup granulated sugar

3 eggs

1 tablespoon vanilla

⅛ teaspoon salt

⅔ cup all-purpose flour, sifted

1½ pounds peaches or nectarines, peeled, pitted, and sliced

1 tablespoon powdered sugar

Preheat oven to 350°. Grease a medium-sized baking dish. Combine the milk, granulated sugar, eggs, vanilla, salt, and flour in a mixing bowl; beat with an electric mixer until the mixture is frothy, about 3 minutes.

Pour enough of the batter into the prepared baking dish to make ¼-inch-deep layer. Bake for 2 minutes. Remove the dish from the oven. Spread the fruit in a layer over cooked batter and pour the remaining batter on top.

Bake until the clafouti is puffed and brown and a knife inserted in the center comes out clean, about 30–35 minutes. Sprinkle with powdered sugar just before serving. Serves 6.

> *Happiness depends, as Nature shows,*
> *Less on exterior things than most suppose.*
>
> —William Cowper

Edible Blossoms

Yes, many flowers (minus stems and leaves) are quite wonderful tasting. But before you start randomly eating flowers from your garden, be sure you know what you are doing—some are deadly poisonous. And of course, if you use pesticides or herbicides in your garden, do not eat unwashed blooms. Caveats aside, flowers do wonderfully in salads, as a garnish to a cold summer soup, as garnishes for serving platters, and to decorate cakes. The following is a list of some of the edible beauties:

Into the Kitchen

    bee balm
    calendula

daylilies

hollyhocks

marigolds

nasturtiums

pansies

roses

scarlet runner bean

sunflowers

violets

Candied Flowers

These delectable treats are easy to create; use them on top of ice cream or cakes. Pick the flowers fresh in the early morning.

violet blossoms

rose petals

1 or 2 egg whites, depending on how many flowers you use

superfine sugar, to taste

Gently wash flowers and pat dry with a clean towel. Beat the egg whites in a small bowl. Pour the sugar into another bowl. Carefully dip the flowers into the egg whites, then roll in sugar, being sure to cover all sides. Set flowers on a cookie sheet and allow to dry in a warm place. Store in a flat container with waxed paper between layers. These will last for several days.

Lemon Tea Bread

Here's a summer treat for those who grow lemon balm.

1 tablespoon finely chopped lemon balm

1 tablespoon finely chopped lemon thyme

³/₄ cup low fat milk

2 cups flour

¹/₄ teaspoon salt

1¹/₂ teaspoons baking powder

6 tablespoons butter, softened

1 cup sugar

2 eggs, beaten

1 tablespoon grated lemon zest

juice of 2 lemons

confectioners' sugar, about ¹/₂–³/₄ cup

Preheat the oven to 325° degrees. Grease a 9 x 5 x 3-inch loaf pan.

In a small saucepan, gently heat the milk with the lemon balm and thyme until just before it boils. Remove from heat and let steep until cool.

Combine the flour, salt, and baking powder in a medium bowl. In a large bowl, cream the butter and sugar together until fluffy. Add the eggs one at a time and beat well. Add the lemon zest, then part of the flour mixture, then some of the milk. Beat well and continue alternating until well combined.

Into the Kitchen

Pour into prepared pan and bake for about 1 hour or until a toothpick inserted into the center comes out clean. While loaf is cooking, place lemon juice in a small bowl with enough confectioners' sugar to make a thick but still pourable glaze. Stir well.

Remove bread from pan and place on a wire rack that has been set over a piece of waxed paper. Pour glaze over top and allow to cool. Makes 1 loaf.

Satisfying Sips

*Y*ou can make all kinds of delicious drinks from the garden. Here are a few recipes to get you started.

Limeade with Rose Water and Peppermint Syrup

Peppermint Syrup:

> ¾ cup water
>
> 1¼ cups super-fine sugar
>
> ½ cup coarsely chopped fresh peppermint
>
> Zest of 1 lemon

Limeade:

> ½ cup lime juice
>
> 2 tablespoons rose water
>
> Fresh peppermint sprigs, for garnish

To make peppermint syrup: Place the water and sugar in a medium saucepan. Bring to a boil, stirring to dissolve the sugar. Add the mint and lemon zest and remove from heat. Allow to cool with the lid on. Strain the mixture, discarding the mint and lemon zest. Makes 1½ cups syrup. (Refrigerate unused portion for future limeades).

To make limeade: Into each of 2 glasses, pour ¼ cup lime juice. Add 1 tablespoon rose water to each glass, stirring well.

Add peppermint syrup to limeade to taste and stir again. Fill glasses with crushed ice. Garnish with fresh peppermint sprigs before serving. Serves 2.

Homemade Ginger Ale

This is very simple to make, but you've got to drink it up after you make it—the carbonation won't last long, and it shouldn't be sealed, or else there could be an explosion.

    3 tablespoons ginger root, peeled
    4 quarts boiling water
    1 lime
    3 cups sugar
    3 tablespoons cream of tartar
    1 tablespoon yeast

Into the Kitchen

Pound the ginger until it is a mash. Pour the boiling water over it, add the lime, sugar, and cream of tartar. Cover with a cloth and let cool to lukewarm. Add yeast; let rest 6 hours. Chill, strain, and serve. Makes 4 quarts.

Unfermented Ginger Ale

This one has no carbonation and can be made in a matter of minutes:

4 ounces ginger root

4 lemons

2 quarts boiling water

2 cups lemon juice

sugar and water to taste

mint leaves, optional

Finely chop the ginger and lemons. Pour boiling water over and steep 5 minutes. Strain out and discard the solids. Chill the liquid. Add lemon juice and sugar to taste; dilute with water if necessary. Serve over ice with mint leaves, if desired. Makes 2 quarts.

Iced Delights

Spice up your ice by adding fruit, herbs, and edible flowers to the ice trays after you've filled them and before freezing. They taste great and add a visual kick to a festive occasion. Here are some fun alternatives to plain old H_2O:

sprigs of rosemary, dill, lemongrass, or mint

roses, carnations, nastursiums, lavender, or pansies

raspberries, blueberries, cucumber, lemon or lime zest

Plenty of Pesto

No book on simple pleasures of the garden would be complete without a pesto recipe. Pesto is usually made with basil (a prolific grower), but can also be made with cilantro or parsley, or a combination. All you need is a large quantity of fresh herbs. Pesto can be frozen and lasts for several months in the freezer. If your basil is going to seed, make a large batch of pesto, minus the cheese, and freeze it. When you use it in the winter, simply add the Parmesan.

¾ cup olive oil

1 clove garlic

1 tablespoon pine nuts

¼ teaspoon salt

⅓ cup grated Parmesan cheese

4 cups basil, cilantro, or parsley, washed

Place all the ingredients except the basil in a food processor. Process until smooth. Add the basil a little at a time, until pesto is smooth. Makes 1 cup.

Into the Kitchen

Preserving Your Bounty

With the invention of the freezer, folks no longer had to can their vegetables from the garden and were able to better preserve both texture and flavor. I remember my mother in the hot days of August starting in the early morning to blanch the zucchini and beans from the garden to freeze for the winter. Now it turns out that many vegetables don't even need to be blanched before freezing. With peas, string beans, cabbage, zucchini, celery, broccoli, onions, and green peppers, you can just clean and cut to size, place in plastic containers with lids, cover with water, and freeze. When completely frozen, remove the block of vegetables from the container, place in a freezer bag and return to the freezer. The downside is that vegetables won't keep as long this way (between 3 and 5 months) but if you aren't doing a tremendous amount, it should work just fine.

Rose Wine

Here's an old fashioned treat. Don't do this if you spray your roses with insecticide. Be sure to thoroughly clean the roses and do not store wine in metal containers or stir with metal utensils; metal reacts to the acid in wine.

2 oranges

3 quarts washed and lightly packed rose petals

1 gallon boiling water

3 pounds sugar

1 package yeast

5 white peppercorns

Rind the oranges and set oranges aside. Cut up rind. Place the rose petals in a large saucepan. Pour the boiling water in and add the orange rind and sugar. Boil for 20 minutes and remove from heat and cool. Add the yeast dissolved in warm water per package instructions, the juice from the oranges, and the peppercorns. Pour into stoneware crock, cover and let sit where temperature is between 60–80° for two weeks. Strain, discard petals, rinds, and peppercorns, and bottle in sterilized jars, corking lightly for about 3 months or until the wine has completed fermenting. To store wine, seal bottles with paraffin. Makes about 1 gallon.

> *Innumerable as the stars of night,*
> *Or stars of morning, dewdrops which the sun*
> *Impearls on every leaf and every flower.*
>
> —Milton

Into the Kitchen

Beautifying Your Home

To pick a flower is so much more satisfying than
just observing it, or photographing it. . . . So in
later years, I have grown in my garden as many
flowers as possible for children to pick.

—Anne Scott-James

Inspired Canvas

I'm a needlework teacher and a needlework judge who also creates her own canvases. My garden is a color garden, and one of the chief pleasures I get out of looking at it is the inspiration it gives me for embroidery. I'm struck by a certain color combination and re-create that in my work.

O the green things growing the green things
growing,
The fair sweet smell of the green things
growing.

—Dinah Mulock Craik

Beautifying Your
Home

Meaningful Stones

*I*nstead of buying gravel or garden rocks, consider collecting what you need from beaches, mountains, river beds, etc. Each hand-selected rock will mean more—and be more beautiful—than a pile of uniform stones.

> *Show me your garden, provided it be your own,*
> *and I will tell you what you are like.*
>
> —Alfred Austin

Boxes of Delight

*W*hen I was in my thirties, I took a grand tour of Europe for a month—in Spain, France, Italy, and Germany. What an introduction to a continent I had read of so longingly all my life. Besides all the glorious food, two things stand out most vividly in my mind: the unbelievable colors of the buildings throughout Italy (the patina of centuries, unreproducable in the United States no matter how hard people try) and the window boxes of geraniums that graced so many homes (the brilliant reds against the dark wood of German houses; the vivid pinks against the ochers, pinks, and peaches of Italian ones). I must say, I gained a real appreciation for geraniums and came home with a passion for window boxes. Unfortunately, like many Americans, I've never lived in a house that has the right kind of windows— what is this prejudice against outer shelves?—so I have had to satisfy my craving with two large wine barrels on my deck. There I keep a crop of petunias perpetually going, although once, in a desire for variety, I put a white begonia in one that is now threatening to take over the entire barrel. Every evening at twilight, I go out to pinch my petunias and contemplate the sunset. It's not Italy, but it's not bad.

> *There is no gardening without humility. Nature is constantly sending even its oldest scholars to the bottom of the class for some egregious blunder.*
>
> —Alfred Austin

Window-Box Basics

The key to colorful window boxes is choosing the right combination of plants. One really effective combination is a single type of flower in just one color: bright yellow begonias, for example, or all red petunias. Or you can try a variety of blue flowers: pale and dark lobelias combined with anchusa capensis is a wonderful combination. Or the tried-and-true pink geraniums with white petunias and variegated ivy. Think also about

Beautifying Your Home

shapes—trailing combined with bushy and upright and foliage—greens break up the arrangement and make it eye catching. Consider where the box is located and choose plants appropriately. If it is in shade all day, be sure all the plants you choose are shade loving. If one type of plant likes a lot of water and another doesn't, it would be best not to plant them together. Purchase enough plants so they can be tightly packed into the box. This will give a lush display when they flower.

To make a window box, make sure there is adequate drainage from the container; if not, drill a couple small holes. Add a layer of broken terra-cotta pieces and then fill with dirt half way. Experiment with placement while plants are still in original containers: tall, upright flowers in the back, trailing ones at front and sides. When you have a pleasing arrangement, water plants thoroughly, then remove from pots and fill dirt to ¾ inch below the rim of the box. Water thoroughly and add soil if necessary.

Be sure to water frequently, even once or twice a day during the hottest weather, and feed with a liquid plant-food once a week. If frequent watering is difficult for you, consider buying a window box with a water reservoir. To keep your box looking lovely, pinch back young plants and prune leggy stems. Deadheading will help plants produce more flowers.

Vacation Tips for Houseplants

While you are away from home, you can make sure that your plants don't end up in the great compost pile in the sky by following these simple tips:

- Before you leave, pull your plants out of hot spots so they will not dry out so quickly and move them to the coolest, darkest spots in your house. Bring any deck plants inside, again to the coolest, darkest locations.

- Do not leave plants in a bucket of water or deep saucer while you are gone. Too much water can rot the roots. Instead, fill trays or saucers with pebbles and water and group plants together to raise humidity; and remember, if the house is closed and lights are off, your plants will need less water.

- If you are going to be gone for any length of time, be sure to have someone come in and water once a week.

> *What continues to astonish me about a garden is that you can walk past it in a hurry, see something wrong, stop to set it right, and emerge an hour or two later breathless, contented, and wondering what on earth happened.*
>
> —Dorothy Gilman

Beautifying Your Home

My Cutting Garden

One of the little things I take true delight in on a regular basis is flower arranging. I'm not good with my hands (my sister used to leave the house in fear when I was learning to sew in junior high), but I have the urge to make something beautiful, and over the years I have discovered that flower arranging is my creative medium. It takes no manual dexterity and, since I planted a cutting garden in my backyard (I can't stand the prices at the florist), no money either. I have an entire cabinet filled with containers (vases I have been given over the years, the beautiful blue bottle a certain type of mineral water comes in, an old jam jar) as well as things scavenged off store-bought bouquets (curly willow, pieces of floral foam, rocks I use to stabilize large arrangements). Every once in a while, I consider actually investing in this passion of mine) buying some floral frogs, getting some vases of certain heights and widths (why, oh why, are the containers I have always too tall or too short or too wide?) But there is something about my low-tech, New England frugal approach that I enjoy, so I continue to make do.

I take great delight in the fact that any time of the year (OK, so I live in California), I can walk outside and find something blooming to liven up my bedroom, the kitchen table, or the shelf in the bathroom. I have never read a book about the principles of flower arranging, and I don't spend too much time on it—maybe five minutes at the most. For me, the joy comes from the ease with which it is possible to make something pleasing to look at: selecting an old yellow mustard jar, filling it with nasturtiums, and placing it on the kitchen table. Ongoing beauty, meal after meal, in only two minutes!

> *A garden is a private world or it is nothing.*
>
> —Eleanor Perényi

Long-Lasting Bouquets

When cutting flowers from the garden, there are a few tricks to gathering them that will ensure long life: (1) be sure to cut them in the early morning or evening. (2) whether using scissors or a sharp knife (there's disagreement over which is better), cut the stems at a deep angle when buds are half open (except for zinnias, marigolds, asters, and dahlias, which should be picked in full bloom), (3) remove leaves at the bottom of the stems (they rot) and plunge flowers immediately up to their necks in tepid water; (4) let sit in a cool place for 4 to 12 hours before arranging.

Certain flowers require different treatment. Daffodils should be kept separate for 12 hours to dry up sap that clogs stems of other flowers. When using tulips or irises, be sure to remove the

Beautifying Your Home

white portion of the stem; only the green part can absorb water. Dip stem ends of poppies and dahlias in boiling water before placing in tepid water to prevent them from oozing a substance that can clog the stems and cause the flowers to wilt.

Paper Cup Lights

*T*hese are great strung on your front porch or out on a deck for a party. The trick is to poke enough of the design in the cup to let the light through, but not to cut it completely.

cut-out patterns

solid colored paper cups

pencil

craft knife

large craft pin (looks like the letter T) or large safety pin

string of small indoor/outdoor Christmas lights

Find in a craft-pattern book or draw your own, a small design that will fit on a paper cup. (A small flower or a star works fine). Cut out the design to make a pattern. Hold the pattern against a cup you have turned upside down, and trace the design lightly onto the side. With the craft knife, cut along sections of the pencil marks and push the cup in a bit along the cut. Do not cut out the design! The little cuts along the pattern will let the light through. With the pin, poke holes along the top and bottom of the design for effect. Punch a hole in the bottom of each cup the size of the Christmas lights and push the bulb through. String up when finished.

> *Every flower about a house certifies to the refinement of somebody. Every vine climbing and blossoming tells of love and joy.*
>
> —Robert Ingersoll

The Romance of Lavender

To me, there is little as wondrous as lavender. I grow at least three varieties at all times and love the shapes each has to offer, distinct yet so easy to know they are bound together as a family. As I wander in my lavender patch, I inhale the oily scent that sticks to my clothes and to my fingers. I'm like a foreigner who returns to a cafe visited long ago; so long ago, he has forgotten its name. One has a small barrel-shaped flower that when dried I keep in a small lace pocket. A scented memory that keeps

Beautifying Your Home

the memory close. Another has a long flower stem that rises up to greet the sky, both day and night. A single bloom to paint the air with its fragrance. The third has a long flower stem that splits into three or four flower bundles, a lamp post for bees searching for honey. All have a scent redolent of foreign travel, of mystery and magic.

> *Nor rural sights alone, but rural sounds,*
> *Exhilarate the spirit, and restore*
> *The tone of languid nature.*
>
> —William Cowper

Luscious Lavender

As a scent, lavender is enjoying huge popularity these days. Maybe because it is considered a romantic yet clean fragrance that is appealing to both men and women, unlike rose, for example, which is associated just with women. Used for centuries to calm nerves, you can enjoy the incomparable scent of lavender in your own home in many ways: bundles of dried lavender, lavender pillows and sachets, and lavender bath products. Lavender is said to be good for sore, tired feet. Simply add a few drops of essential oil to a basin and place feet in water.

One incredibly easy thing to do is to buy lavender essential oil and scent your closet or chest of drawers by placing the oil on a cotton ball and rubbing it along the insides of wooden drawers and shelves. The wood will slowly release the fragrance.

Lavender Bouteille

*T*his is a woven lavender wand (*bouteille* means bottle in French) used as a sachet to scent closets and underwear drawers. You can make an elaborate one that is woven like a basket, but I prefer the simplest possible.

> 40 long stalks of freshly cut lavender, picked at the height of bloom
>
> twine or raffia
>
> beautiful ribbon, optional

Gather the stalks together into one big bunch. Remove any side shoots and tie together tightly just under the flowers with the twine or raffia. Bend down all the stalks evenly over the lavender blossoms and tie with twine again. Even off the ends with scissors. If you like, you can use a decorative ribbon at the end. To release the scent, simply squeeze the bouteille.

Beautifying Your Home

Heavenly Hydrangeas

*H*ydrangeas, those pink, blue, and white wonders, are hot these days, so popular that police in California are reporting that the blooms are being stolen from people's yards. (My hydrangea problem is of the four-legged variety; deer keep eating the buds before they open). If you have some of your own, late summer, when the blossoms have just started to dry on the bush but before the color has faded, is the time to harvest for drying.

Getting perfect, colorful, full, fluffy dried heads isn't completely easy, however. Flower experts report only about a 50 percent success rate, so it's best to start with a lot of flowers. Lacecap hydrangeas are particularly difficult; try the mop-head varieties instead. The trick is to remove all leaves and recut the stems as soon as you get into the house. Then hold the stems over a flame for 20 seconds, then submerge in cold water up to the flower head for 2 days. Pour off all but ½ inch of water and let the rest evaporate in a warm dry place, such as next to your water heater. When the water is gone, the blooms should be dry.

Patience is a flower that grows not in everyone's garden.

—English proverb

Nourishing Body and Soul

*Summer is the time when one sheds one's tensions
with one's clothes, and the right kind of day is
jeweled balm for the battered spirit. A few of
those days and you can become drunk with the
belief that all's right with the world.*

—Ada Louise Huxtable

Morning Ritual

It's 8:30 A.M. and I am due at the clinic for work at nine. But first it's time for my daily stroll out to the garden. Standing among vegetables ringed by flowers, I get lost in a reverie: wouldn't it be wonderful to be able to talk with the bees who by the dozens visit the dahlias and oregano that's flowering—or at least track them as to where their hive is.

Suddenly, I am captivated by some damaged tomato vines speckled with the tell-tale signs of tomato hornworm catepillar poop. These grotesque creatures are hard to find as they are well camouflaged, like Japanese theatre puppets. But I am determined to ferret them out before they do any more damage. Ah, there's one! Over the fence with you. And another, and yet another.

*Nourishing Body
& Soul*

With a start, I realize a half hour has passed; once again I have lost track of time. Isn't that the most delicious garden feeling?

> *Earth and sky, wind and trees, rivers and fields,*
> *the mountains and the sea. All are excellent*
> *schoolmasters and teach some of us more than we*
> *could ever learn from books.*
>
> —Anonymous

Salt Glow

This is fabulous for exfoliating dead skin, particularly when your tan is starting to flake. Be sure not to use on your face or neck; it's too rough for that.

2 cups sea salt

7 drops of your favorite essential oil

1 ounce sweet almond oil

Place salt and oils in a bowl and combine well with your fingers. Stand or sit naked in an empty bathtub and rub salt mixture into your skin with your hands, starting with your feet. Massage in a circular motion. As the salts fall, pick up and re-use until you reach your neck. Then fill the tub with warm water and soak.

Peaches and Cream Moisturizer

Blend together in a blender or a food processor one peach and enough heavy cream to create a spreadable consistency. Massage onto your skin when needed. Refrigerate unused portion. (And use up within a day or so or it will "turn.")

Facial Toner

This is a really easy, all-natural skin freshener, a perfect pick-me-up for hot, humid weather.

1½ cups witch hazel extract

½ cup rose water

1 tablespoon grated lime peel

1 tablespoon dried rosemary leaves

2 drops lavender oil

2 drops rosemary oil

Combine the witch hazel and rose water in a clean glass jar with a tight-fitting lid. Shake well to thoroughly combine. Add the remaining ingredients and again shake well, this time for fiveminutes. Store the jar in a dark, cool place, shaking five minutes a day for two weeks. At the end of that period, strain the mixture and store the remaining liquid in an airtight container, where it will last up to six weeks if refrigerated. For extra refreshment, try keeping a spritz bottle full of toner, and use it straight from the refrigerator.

Nourshing Body & Soul

Skin Soother Bath

This wonderful recipe will soothe any skin condition, from heat rash to chicken pox. It's wonderful for your skin and hair, so use it even when you're problem-free!

½ cup finely ground oatmeal

1 cup virgin olive oil

2 cups aloe vera gel

20 drops rosemary or lavender oil

Combine the ingredients in a large bowl; stir well. Add to a warm, running bath.

Citrus Toner

¼ cup lemon peel, finely grated

¼ cup grapefruit, finely grated

1 cup mint leaves

1 cup water

Add mint and citrus peelings to rapidly boiling water. Continue to boil for 1–2 minutes or until peels become soft and slightly translucent. Remove from heat. Cool and strain. Store in the refrigerator or freezer; this will last 2–3 weeks.

Weeding Therapy

When three things go wrong by midmorning, there's only one thing to do: Head for the garden. The beans needed weeding. Great; something to work out my resentments on. I knelt and started; the lamb's-quarters and pigweed pulled out easily, so I ripped them out angrily, in big handfuls. That felt good. After a few minutes I was enjoying the comforting feel of the soft, warm earth. I noticed the tiny beans were coming along just as they should, in elegant clusters hanging straight down.

As the weed heap grew and the row of handsome, weed-free plants extended behind me, I realized I wasn't frowning anymore; actually I was smiling. . .

Is gardening therapeutic? You bet it is.

A Hatful of Beauty

For a summer garden party, beautify your old straw hat with a ribbon of fresh flowers. All you need besides the hat is raffia, scissors, and some flowers. Try flowers that will last a long time

Nourshing Body & Soul

out of water—sunflowers, statice, yarrow, chrysanthemums, carnations, and daisies are best, as are sturdy greens like sword ferns. Cut the greens and flowers with long enough stems to bundle. Separate each kind and create hand-size bunches of each. Set aside. Cut several strands of raffia long enough to not only go around the hat's crown, but wrap around the flower bundles. Knot the strands together at one end. Starting 6 inches from the knotted end, twist the raffia around the stems of one bunch of flowers several times. Lay the next bunch down as far apart from the previous bunch as you like, and repeat the wrapping process Continue down the length of raffia until you have a garland long enough to go around the hat. Place the garland on the hat and tie the two ends of raffia together; tuck any loose raffia under the flowers. To keep fresh for several days, store hat in the refrigerator in a plastic bag.

Simplicity is the essence of happiness.

—Cedric Bledsoe

A Wake-up Call

I was standing in our community garden looking at the collossal collection of cantaloupe that I had grown—my first-ever attempt. Vistas of an alternative career opened—I would leave my career as a physician and become a champion cantaloupe farmer! (Little did I know this was one of life's "fabulous firsts." That day was over twenty years ago and since that time I've not successfully grown even one more).

As I stood relishing my achievement, out of the corner of my eye I spotted a lovely teenage girl in a nearby plot. She was staking up some tomato plants. She was a patient of mine, a schizophrenic. She had her head cocked, listening intently. There was a relaxed smile on her face, and I realized that in this peaceful place, she was not hearing her usual voices of terror. She was listening to the whisper of the winds and the song of the birds. I left quietly.

Natural Headache Remedies

*H*ere are two ways to handle a headache with ingredients from the garden. The first is a midwestern pioneer recipe; the second is an old-fashioned German cure.

Headache Pillow

Nourishing Body & Soul

½ ounce ground cloves

2 ounces dried lavender

2 ounces dried marjoram

2 ounces dried rose petals

2 ounces detony rose leaf

1 teaspoon orris root

2 pieces of cotton batting, slightly smaller than a handkerchief

2 handkerchiefs

lace or ribbon, optional

Grind spices, flowers, and orris root together, either by hand with a mortar and pestle or in the food processor. Pack the powder in between the two pieces of cotton. Sew together three sides of the two handkerchiefs. Place the cotton "pillow" inside and hand sew the fourth side tight enough that the contents don't leak out. Decorate with lace or ribbons, if desired. To use, lie on pillow and inhale fragrance or place over eyes.

> *As an instrument of planetary home repair, it is
> hard to imagine anything as safe as a tree.*
>
> —Jonathan Weiner

Headache Remedy

1 quart white rose petals

1 quart jar, sterilized

about 1 quart 90 proof vodka or rubbing alcohol

Pack the jar with the rose petals. Pour the vodka over and let stand, covered, for at least 24 hours. Rub on forehead, temples, and back of neck.

When You Water, Water

Every year the sitting area on my deck shrinks as I buy more pots and fill them with summer flowers. I water them slowly, pot by pot. Once in a while, I try to do two things at once—water and talk on the phone. But it's distracting to pay attention to the person at the other end while I'm watching the water flow into the rich brown soil and smiling at the flowers. So by the beginning of July, I just let the phone ring when I'm watering.

As each plant soaks up the wet nourishment, I stand amid the air, the smells, and the sounds of life, and all of them help to slow my world down, quiet my thoughts, and give me time to pause.

Lavender Bath Oil

Here's another great way to relax—an aromatherapy bath.

1 cup almond or grapeseed oil

½ teaspoon lavender essential oil

¼ teaspoon vitamin E oil

dried lavender sprigs

10 ounce decorative bottle with a top

ribbon and gift tag, if desired

Nourshing Body & Soul

Combine the oils in a glass container and test the scent on your skin. (You might want to add a bit more of one thing or another depending on the fragrance). Place the lavender sprigs into the bottle. Using a funnel, pour the oil into the bottle and close the top. Store in cool, dry place.

His Soul Walked with Flowers

*M*y father was an ambitious man, though not in the usual way. His garden of beautiful roses was important to him, but most of all, he wanted, with all of his heart, to grow a seven-headed sweet pea. To his knowledge, this had never been done before.

The harsh climate and stony soil of the northeast coast of England was more conducive to the production of stalwart vegetables, coarse in quality but gargantuan in size. Local gardeners competed in shows for the biggest and best. My father was a different kind of dreamer. His soul walked with flowers.

We lived in a dirty, decaying city grappling with the decline of shipbuilding and coal mining. Our small red brick house was skirted on three sides by the tiniest of gardens, its perimeters defined by the ubiquitous privet hedge. Reluctant sun struggled through the constant, dour overcast of clouds and was mostly blocked by nearby buildings. Did he not realize that roses needed sunshine? Then there were the cutting arctic winds, icy as snow stars, that keened year round through every crevice.

They blew the hope out of such fragile blooms as sweet peas. As I said, he was a dreamer, utterly convinced that a seven-headed flower could be coaxed from his plants, not by the technicalities of cross-fertilization, but by sheer love and devotion.

Our neighbors—if they had gardens at all—had geometric patches of grass bordered by regimental rows of marigolds and snapdragons. His was a rock garden with cascading lobelia and alyssium, sheltered by a richly hued copper birch tree. Then there was the rose bed, each plant named with pride of place, leading to his favorite, the exotic, heavily scented Crimson Glory. And there was the bed of sweet peas, each plant supported by elaborate scaffolding. Everything flourished.

My father held his ambition lightly. He was a buoyant personality, funny, teasing. It was the process of gardening that delighted him. With the diligence and dedication of an acolyte, he was out daily, fumbling with loving but clumsy hands at the delicate tendrils of the sweet peas as he cajoled them into climbing further up their supporting frames.

He nourished them with more than love alone. The manure heap sat by the kitchen door. There was nowhere else for it to go. It was supplemented by steaming pails of fresh droppings from the horse-drawn produce, fish, and coal carts that delivered to our street. Fly papers flapped from the kitchen ceiling. Mother yelled to keep the door shut. We children laughed at his zeal with an exaggerated holding of our noses. He was oblivious,

Nourshing Body & Soul

his sense of self lost but reflected fantastically in the possible.

This continued throughout the dream of my childhood years. When there wasn't much food on the table, there would always be small bowls of flowers and tiny bouquets went daily to the neighbors.

Inevitably, it happened. One day we were all called out to see the pale lavender, gossamer seven-headed sweet pea. Its photograph was ceremoniously taken. With utmost tenderness, my father brought it into the house, surrounding it with maidenhair fern and reverently placing it in a vase at the center of the table. Never have I seen a man so blissful, so content. But only now, sixty years later, can I fully appreciate his moment, his total lack of self-limitation.

I've had many gardens, big and small. Now, in my old age, I have only a tiny deck. It's overflowing with an abundance of flowers, all a little out of control. My children laugh at my "jungle," the lack of space to move around, but I know that two of them are avid gardeners. The blistering sun and brassy blue skies of California cruelly discourage sweet peas. But there are the roses, masses of them in pots, among them the exotic, sweetly scented Crimson Glory. Now there's a memory.

Fall

The harvest moon has no innocence,
like the slim quarter moon of a spring twilight,
nor has it the silver penny brilliance of the moon
that looks down upon the resorts of summer time.
Wise, ripe, and portly, like an old Bacchus,
it waxes night after night.

—Donald Culross Peattie

In the Garden

A solitary maple on a woodside flames in single scarlet, recalls nothing so much as the daughter of a noble house dressed for a fancy ball, with the whole family gathered round to admire her before she goes.

—Henry James

Attracting the Birds

I was at my parents' home on Cape Cod last October and became mesmerized by the chickadees, juncos, and finches that came right up to the dining room window to eat from feeders attached by suction cups to the glass. I've always had bird feeders, but they were hung from trees quite a way from the house and, so, while I had the inner satisfaction of doing a good deed, my eyes missed out on the pleasure of the darting creatures themselves. So I decided when I returned home to try and lure the birds to the window. I learned a bit in the process.

First, the best time to start is late fall, because the cold weather makes birds more anxious to find food and therefore more willing to try something new. Birds' body temperatures are

In the Garden

on average ten degrees warmer than humans, and they need an almost constant food supply to stay alive. The cold weather slows down and kills the insects they eat and so they must find an alternate food supply.

It doesn't matter which side of the house you put the feeders on, but it should be protected from the wind. You should have a good view, but it shouldn't be so active in the room that the birds are scared off all the time. At my parents, birds would come when we were all sitting down quietly, but every time someone moved close to the window, they would scatter. A feeder on a pole in full view of the window but back a little turned out to be the best compromise at my house. The birds felt safer than right at the window, and I could still see them (plus cats and squirrels couldn't get the birds or seed.) As for the food, wildbird seed mix is fine, as is cracked chick feed mixed with sunflower seeds for the seed-eating birds. Bug eaters such as woodpeckers shy away from seeds, but love suet; you can buy special suet feeders at any bird or nature store.

Down the Garden Path

Whenever I arrive in my garden, "I make the tour." Is this a personal idiosyncrasy, or do all good gardeners do it?

It would be interesting to know. By "making the tour," I mean only that I step from the front window, turn to the right, and make an infinitely detailed examination of every foot of ground, every shrub and tree, walking always over an appointed course.

There are certain very definite rules to be observed when you are "making the tour." The chief rule is that you must never take anything out of its order. You may be longing to see if a crocus has come out in the orchard, but it is strictly forbidden to look before you have inspected all the various beds, bushes, and trees that lead up to the orchard.

You must not look at the bed ahead before you have finished with the bed immediately in front of you. You may see, out of the corner of your eye, a gleam of strange and unsuspected scarlet in the next bed but one, but you must steel yourself against rushing to this exciting blaze, and you must stare with cool eyes at the earth in front, which is apparently blank, until you have made certain that it is not hiding anything. Otherwise, you will find that you rush wildly round the garden, discover one or two sensational events, and then decide that nothing else has happened.

I would rather sit on a pumpkin and have it all to myself, then be crowded on a velvet cushion.

—Henry David Thoreau

In the Garden

Snail Patrol

I am a person who tries to live up to the admonition "thou shalt not kill." From fellow humans to squirrels to even ants, I would rather try and bother an animal into changing its behavior than end its life. (The proof of my imperfection in this arises from how much I enjoy a good cut of beef or roast lamb. But that's another tale.)

As many gardeners know, when the summer heat begins to pass into the cool, wet fall, our friend the snail makes his annual food pilgrimage to many beloved plants. There are a number of ways to try and control the slimy one. For small pots, plots, and raised beds, copper tape has a slight electric current that will suggest a different meal. For larger areas, one can find many ways to kill a snail. If you happen to live near any open area as I do, I suggest flying lessons.

For me, the easiest time to search for emerging escargot is early in the morning as I go out to retrieve the morning paper. The garden is still fairly damp, and they are finishing up their meal. I bring an empty plastic container with me and collect all the snails I can find. Then moving to the side of my driveway I pick them out one by one and give them their first flight into the wild grass on the other side.

As time goes on, I find fewer and fewer little helmeted ones. Maybe the first solo has scared them to death (I hope not), or maybe they have gotten my hint. I can't say for sure, but the days of finding a plant almost completely consumed by our friend, the snail, are gone.

> *Tickle it with a hoe and it will laugh into a*
> *harvest.*
>
> —English proverb

Exotic Lettuce Mixes

Are you a buyer of those expensive (four to six dollars a pound) mixed salad greens? You can easily make your own mix by buying lettuce seeds such as Oakleaf, Black Seeded Simpson, Red Salad Bowl, as well as, arugula, mizuna, watercress, and chicory. In many parts of the country, it is too hot for lettuce during the summer; these do best in the cooler weather of fall and spring. But you can keep them growing even during the summer if you plant new seedlings every couple of weeks and provide a "roof" made of shade cloth you can buy at any garden supply store. The trick is to harvest when the leaves are very young and tender, otherwise they may be too bitter. When the plants are a couple inches high, sheer the tops with scissors for your salad; they will grow back quickly, and you'll have salads for weeks.

In the Garden

Bittersweet Memories

I haven't lived on the East Coast for twenty years, but I still remember with great fondness the bittersweet. When the weather had that particular tang in the air signaling it was headed towards cold and the leaves had mostly fallen, there it was— shockingly bright-orange berries sitting in tiny red cups on dark brown branches. I'd come across it by surprise at the edge of the woods or in a neighbor's yard; I could never remember seeing it at any other time of the year. Whether it flowered, what the leaves were like, I couldn't say. It seemed to appear just for fall, as a feast for the birds (and for my eyes) before the long, cold winter.

> *You can count the number of apples on one tree,*
> *but you can never count the number of trees in*
> *one apple.*
>
> —Anonymous

Clothesline Lyric

I don't suppose a clothesline would strike most of us as an especially fascinating object to visit, but our clothesline is a lovely spot. First there is the long row of herbs: summery savory, and sweet marjoram sending up pungent drifts of fragrance; basil and tarragon joining with orange bergamot, peppermint, and parsley for a whole bouquet of flavorsome scents.

The apricot-colored, full-petaled Angels Mateu, sweetest rose in the garden, perfumes the air with its delicious fresh raspberry scent, while nearby Audie Murphy's wealth of spicy red blooms make one brilliant bouquet.

As I raise my head to hang the sheets, there on the hill above sits the resident red-tailed hawk perched on the power tower looking for field mice—maybe a small snake for breakfast? Sometimes he soars over me, swooping close to my clothesline so I can see clearly his squinting eye, the broad rust-tail, the streaked belly. He has lived, or perhaps it's his ancestors who have been with us ever since we built here, twenty-eight years ago, doing his thing to keep the mouse population in perspective.

I wonder if he recognizes me as I do him. Goodness knows he's seen me often enough, scrambling around this hill. I wonder what a hawk's eye view of me is like, tied down to the earth here, as he soars effortlessly on broad buteo wings on rising air currents.

In the Garden

Faint chitterings and then a little burst of melody comes from behind me, and, as I turn, a puff of gauzy thistle fluff floats up from the big clump of purple thistles by my fence. I can't see the singer, but again come the chittering notes, much like the noise of milk bottles (who remembers milk bottles?) jarring together.

Ah, now I can see them, a pair of lesser (dark-blacked) goldfinches, already in their dull new fall plumage. Just last month they were golden, now they are olive green. Goldfinches are among the sweetest singers, sounding a bit like the canary, to which they are distantly related. These little fellows have been busy!

All along the base of the fence are gossamer drifts of thistle-down, catching the sun to shimmer like silk. How quickly they work over the ripening thistle heads, the small dark seeds rich in nourishing oil. We'll have lesser goldfinches with us all winter but not necessarily these individuals. In large flocks many migrate to southern California, Central America, and as far south as Peru, where the weed seeds ripen all winter (their summer).

From up in the orchard, perhaps from the green gage plum tree, come the practice trills of the teenage house finches. They'll be on their way south soon, too, with the rest of their flock. I don't begrudge them some plums to store up the needed energy. They'll return with our spring, accomplished singers to warble their thanks.

Our clothesline is a lovely spot.

A Surprising Development

I have always grown flowers and houseplants, so when I moved into my new house two springs ago, I was a bit taken aback by the large yard. The former owners were clearly not flower people; not a bloom in sight. They had planted fruit trees everywhere—several varieties of apple, an apricot, pear, cherry, and fig, and at least two kinds of plums. My first instinct was to pull them out and plant a flower bed. (The fact that they were all lined up in a row along the back fence and pressed up against the house didn't help in terms of aesthetic appeal either.) But I couldn't imagine killing a tree and had other priorities that took my time and so by midsummer found myself the proud owner of hundreds of green plums. Tart on the outside, with an orange, almost pumpkin-colored, sweet flesh inside, they quickly became my heart's desire. By fall, when my Macintosh apples, Bartlett pears, and figs were ripe, I was hooked. Completely organic, perfectly ripe fruit—oh, the blush on the Mac, the glow on the Bartlett—at my fingertips; it was a veritable Garden of Eden. Add to that the blossoms of spring that brightened many a grey day, and I had become a rabid tree owner.

But flowers were still on my mind, so I figured out a compromise. We moved a few of the smaller trees, gave away several to fruit-loving friends, and ultimately had to sacrifice only one plum tree in order to have my flowers and eat my fruit too.

In the Garden

A *Walter Mitty Mood*

I'm sitting in my garden in a Walter Mitty mood. I am the creator of a world—a luscious tomato, a creamy butternut squash, a thirst-quenching cucumber. I created these by planting little seeds—no store-bought plants in my world. Admittedly, I got an assist from the First Creator who caused the sun to shine and the gentle rain to fall upon my plantings. As did the First, I looked at my creation and saw that it was good.

Weather Signs

According to folklore, it will be a hard winter if

there is an unusually large crop of acorns;

heavy moss appears on the north side of trees;

grape leaves turn color early in the season;

corn has thick husks;

hornets have triple-insulated nests;

cattle get rough coats and rabbits and squirrels have heavier fur than usual;

wooly bear caterpillars are black all over. If dark only in the middle, only midwinter will be hard; if the ends are darker, the beginning and end of the winter will be hard.

Walking to the Compost Pile

We make an earnest effort to compost our kitchen waste, specifically coffee grounds, chopped-up banana skins, and other biodegradable gunk. As the compost heap is at the very back of our yard, every morning after breakfast I wander out with a cutting board full of goodies for the little red worms. This trip necessitates a journey through the garden, and that means a step into slowed-down time.

There's always something new poking up through the adobe, or starting to leaf or bloom, or growing where it shouldn't, or just trimmed picturesquely with frost. For a gardener—even a hit or miss one like me—a walk through one's garden is almost guaranteed to provide a meditative change of pace.

In search of my mother's garden, I found my own.

—Alice Walker

In the Garden

Compost Considerations

Most gardeners feel that fall is the best time to start a compost heap, when leaves and other green clippings and debris are readily available. To begin, place an eight-inch thick, even layer of wood materials, such as wood chips, sawdust, shredded newspaper, or small twigs and branches on the bottom of your compost bin (this can be any homemade or store-bought container, at least four-feet high and five-feet square with adequate but not excessive aeration, which will not be easily disturbed by woodland critters and household pets). On top of the wood layer, place an equal amount of green materials; grass clippings, leaves, fruit or vegetable peelings, coffee and tea grounds, wilted cut flowers, and the like. You should never include animal flesh or by-products, eucalyptus or black walnut leaves, and anything treated with pesticides or chemicals. Gradually add enough water to make the entire contents of your compost container damp but not wet. Thoroughly mix the two layers with a long-handled shovel or rake. As new materials accumulate, they may be added; just take care to ensure that neither woods nor greens reach too high a concentration.

In approximately twelve to sixteen weeks, your compost is ready for garden use. Always take what you need from the bottom of the bin. (This will be the richest compost.)

> *And forget not that the earth delights to feel*
> *your bare feet and the wind longs to play with*
> *your hair.*
>
> —Kahlil Gibran

Spigot Solution

Ever wonder what to do with all those slivers of soap besides throwing them away? I slip them into the leg of an old pair of pantyhose, clip the leg off, and tie it to my spigot outside. I save the slivers and have a convenient place to wash my hands after gardening.

In the Garden

With Family and Friends

He who shares the joy in what he's grown
spreads joy abroad and doubles his own.

—Anonymous

Kitty Quality Time

It's early morning and I'm out doing a little weeding and watering accompanied by my three cats. They love to play "big kitty in the jungle" when I'm out in the yard, following me and my hose around. Callahan proudly brings me a bunch of sourgrass I've just pulled, the way other cats bring their owners dead mice. I tell him dogs have peed on it, but that doesn't diminish his pleasure. The sun shines, the cats stalk, and all is right in my world.

The blueberry is nature's compensation for the
ruin of forest fires. It grows best where the woods
have been burned away and the soil is too poor to
raise another crop of trees.

—Henry Van Dyke

With Family
& Friends

Plant Memories

I've been a houseplant owner since I was in college in the early '70s. I'm not sure why, but when other students were smoking dope and dropping acid, my boyfriend and I were making terrariums out of old gallon wine bottles and battling mealy bugs with alcohol-soaked Q-tips. I still have some of the plants from those days and most of the others I've gathered over the past twenty-five years (I have had a few failures), because I can't seem to purposely give up on a plant.

Indeed, the only plant I ever abandoned was a ficus I had bought with my significant other at the very beginning of our fourteen year relationship. In the glow of new love, we proclaimed it "our" tree and, in retrospect, it did mirror our relationship quite accurately: lush and green in the beginning, then dropping most of its leaves somewhere along the way, languishing but never quite dying. I guess you could consider it mercy killing when my S.O. came to me one day to say it was over. I took all the plants but that one, and it quickly died. To this day, I can't abide a ficus in my house.

I guess I take my plants seriously, although I certainly don't spend a lot of time taking care of them. But their meaning to me must come across to others. The most scared I have ever seen my stepchildren was when, at age eight and ten, during a roughhousing session in the living room, they broke a very old Christmas cactus of mine. It was no big deal as far as I was concerned, but they were so wide-eyed and ashen you would think I was about to kill them over it.

Now, as I wander through my house, the decades come streaming back: the revived Christmas cactus ten years later, blooming so vigorously that you could never guess it had ever been in pieces; the spider plant I inherited in the '80s when my former boyfriend moved back to the East Coast and I mourned for seven years; the creeping charlie from my commune days in the '70s when I sunbathed naked in the courtyard and managed to avoid joining in the revolving bed game; the philodendron my parents sent when I bought my first house, grown so large now it must be staked to the wall, which has survived three moves; the verdant hoya my new husband and I bought as we wait for our baby to arrive. So much life, so many different lives. I can barely believe I'm the same person, but here they are, silent green witnesses to it all.

> *It is only when you start to garden—probably after fifty—that you realize something important happens every day.*
>
> —Geoffrey B. Charlesworth

With Family & Friends

The Bridal Wreath

*T*here was a sadly neglected corner of my parents' yard that had an ancient bedraggled shrub my mother called the bridal wreath. I thought this eyesore was undeserving of such a poetic name since it hardly produced even a handful of white buds and seemed to have a blackberry bush rapidly overtaking it. I had recently learned the fine art of pruning and decided one late fall afternoon to try it on this tired old shrub. I really went at it with the shears and, with the help of my father, got rid of the blackberry invader and hacked away until not much was left of the venerable old bridal wreath. I remember my mother nearly cried when she saw the havoc we had wrought; her mother had planted this plant fifty years before. I told her not to worry and to wait to see what happened.

It sat there all fall and winter, pretty much forgotten. Then, one early spring day, we all had the most wonderful surprise— the bridal wreath had turned into a showpiece overnight with dozens of sprays of perfect white flowers that lasted for weeks. My mother was happiest of all. Evidently, the bridal wreath had been her mother's pride and joy and was now fully restored to its former glory. It was amazingly beautiful. The sprays were indeed perfect for a bride's crown.

In Memory

I was about ten years old when I asked my mother, "Why do you give people flowers when they die? Why not do it when they are alive?" This was at the annual decoration that took place at the church cemetery where my father was buried. She thoughtfully explained that the flowers are for the living. They are a symbol that we offer to sweetly remember the people we love who we have lost, and, by presenting the flowers, we have an occasion to congregate, remember, and talk about our loved ones. I noticed that day that my Aunt Suzie had brought flowers from her own garden instead of the usual florist sprays. Her arrangement was a profusion of sweet william and cockscomb carefully, yet naturally, arranged in a coffee tin she disguised in cellophane. The flowers reminded me of my father—a down-to-earth man who enjoyed working outside in his garden or tinkering with his tractor. Their deep crimson colors mirrored his favorite color—burgundy—the color of his only sport coat, his last truck, even the trim on our house shutters and door. My mother was right. Those flowers were for the living.

> *For in the true nature of things, if we will rightly consider, every green tree is far more glorious than if it were made of gold and silver.*
>
> —Martin Luther

With Family & Friends

Trading Pleasure

Start a bulb-and-seed exchange with friends. When you are doing your harvesting in the fall—dividing bulbs and drying out seeds for next year—try trading with friends for a no-cost way to increase the variety in your garden. We started doing this years ago when we found out the hard way that a packet of zucchini seeds was far too many for two people to plant and eat. We divided them up among our friends around the country and that got the ball rolling.

To send bulbs, place them in a paper bag and then in a box. To collect seeds, shake the flower heads over an empty glass jar. To send seeds, take a small piece of paper and make a little envelope out of it by folding it in half. Take each side and fold in about ½ inch toward middle. Tape those two sides, place the seeds inside the opening at the top and then fold top down and tape again. Write on the outside what is inside, and mail in a padded envelope. A sweet surprise for family or friends.

> *A violet, by a mossy stone*
> *Half hidden from the eye!*
> *Fair as a star, when only one*
> *Is shining in the sky.*
>
> —William Wordsworth

Cactus Garden

A perfect gift for those who want plants but kill others from lack of water. Find a low ceramic pot or bowl and plant a few different varieties of cacti. You might want to add a pretty rock or dried flowers for color (red celosia is a wonderful choice). Handling a cactus is not painful if you wrap a towel around it several times and use the towel like a noose to lift it out of the old pot and into the new. Rather than your fingers, use a spoon to pack dirt around roots.

> *I am spending delightful afternoons in my garden,*
> *watching everything living around me. As I grow*
> *older, I feel everything departing, and I love*
> *everything with more passion.*
>
> —Emile Zola

Onion and Garlic Braids

I love to grow onions and garlic just so that I can braid them into garlands and give them away for Christmas presents. All you have to do in preparation is to be sure to leave on the long tops when you harvest your crop. It's just like braiding hair. Cut a piece of twine as long as you want your braid and lay it down

**With Family
& Friends**

on a table. Line up the onions or garlic in a row on the twine with the leaves all facing toward you, each onion or garlic bulb slightly overlapping the one before. Starting with the first at the top of the line, separate the leaves into three sections, incorporating the twine into one of the sections, and braid as you would hair. When you are about half way down the length of the first bulb's leaves, begin to incorporate the second bulb's leaves so that the bulb sits on top of the previous braid. Continue until you reach the end of the bulbs. Dry in the sun for 3–5 days and then they are ready for hanging as decorations—and to use. Simply snip off the last one on the braid as needed.

Great Gift

Tie up a package of sunflower seeds with a ribbon and a sunflower.

Gardening Cohorts

I'm part of a group of eight friends who live in surrounding towns and have gotten together at least once a month for the past four years. We find we often function like old-fashioned barn-raising neighbors—when someone needs to move, we're all there hauling boxes; we have summer solstice celebrations together and sixtieth birthday celebrations and adoption parties. A lot of our sharing is around our gardens. When a massive oak in our yard died, we divided the firewood among us; when a rhododendron bush needed lifting up, the rhododendron expert among us was in charge. We swap trees, give produce, offer orchids, help out when it's time to weed or harvest, trade recipes, and visit nurseries together. Nothing unusual, except in this fast-paced, mobile, urban life when neighbors seem to come and go in the blink of an eye, it's the kind of connection that I find all too rarely. No reason to be together, except the sharing of the dailiness of life on an on-going basis. A lot like nature. Very ordinary, but profoundly important.

> *Remember that the most beautiful things in the world are the most useless; peacocks and lilies for instance.*
>
> —John Ruskin

Worm Garden

With Family & Friends

*T*his is an activity more likely to be enjoyed by the little ones. Fill a gallon glass jar with alternating layers of sand and garden soil until it is almost full. Then add compost items such a coffee grounds, banana peels cut into pieces, old dried leaves, etc. Place about ten worms on the top and cover with a piece of black cloth. Whenever curiosity strikes, remove the cloth for a few minutes and see what the worms are up to. When interest wanes, return worms to the garden.

Legacy of Trees

O ur family has decided to plant three trees, representing our three family members, in each of the fifty states. The places we're picking are all places that contain either our last name or one of our first names. We're doing it because we believe planting trees is a way to help protect and beautify nature, as well as provide habitat for birds and animals. So far we've done twenty states and have been received graciously in each town. We generally find a family that is willing to have us plant a tree in their yard, but we've also done a few street trees.

I lie amid the Goldenrod
I love to see it lean and nod.

—Mary Elemmer

In Aunt Ruth's Garden

As a child, I was fortunate enough to have an aunt who loved to garden. She had a beautiful old-fashioned garden in the Ohio valley with many plants that had been handed down through generations of my family. I can still smell the lilac from a bush that was over one hundred years old and home to many bees. When I was barely old enough to toddle along behind her, Aunt Ruth would show me her tricks of the trade—rooting, transplanting, deadheading, even grafting.

I quickly learned that, by admiring one of my aunt's flowers heartily, I would usually be given a seedling, a cutting, or a whole plant. In her infinite wisdom, she decided that I could be taught the craft of gardening and help her clean and thin some beds at the same time. This became a marvelous arrangement that persisted well into my adulthood until I moved 3000 miles away to a different "zone." Now, as a city dweller, my dream is to have a little garden patch of my own where I can carry on the family tradition.

With Family & Friends

Into the Kitchen

*For all things produced in a garden, whether of
salads or fruits, a poor man will eat better that
has one of his own, than a rich man that has
none.*

—J. C. Loudoun

An Apple a Day

Everyone in my family is a dried-fruit fanatic, but the cost of
the store-bought variety makes my hair stand on end. So
I've learned how to dry my own apples. This year our apple tree
seems like it will have enough to spare, but most years I just go
to a farm stand and buy a few bushels. (They really shrink down
when they dry.) Just core and peel your favorite variety. Slice
about ¼-inch thick. As you cut, place pieces in a pot of water
that has ¼ cup of lemon juice in it to prevent browning while
you are working. Place slices in a single layer on a wire rack and
bake at 225° for a few hours, turning occasionally. Dry until they
are leathery; time will vary. Be sure to store in an airtight
container.

Into the Kitchen

Bursts of Flavor

My husband is a rabid tomato-grower. After our enthusiasm for freshly picked and eaten cherry tomatoes has waned and fall has arrived, then it's time for sun-dried tomatoes. Though I have actually dried tomatoes in the sun, a much more dependable and efficient method is to dry them in an oven for 5–8 hours, depending on the size of the fruit. After cleaning and splitting the tomatoes in half, I salt them lightly on oiled cookie pans and place them in a 170° oven. When they are dry but not crispy, I pack jars with the tomatoes and fill to the top with extra virgin olive oil (press with a spoon to make sure the air is all out and add more oil if needed to cover tomatoes completely). We have so many we give lots away, but I always save some for ourselves. In the middle of winter these make the quickest and sweetest tomato paste in the world.

> *More than anything, I must have flowers, always, always.*
>
> —Claude Monet

Chicken with Sun-Dried Tomatoes

This recipe never fails to get raves at parties large and small. It's simple, once you get the hang of the rolling-up process. I pound the chicken with a full wine bottle, but you can use a flat mallet instead.

4 skinless, boneless chicken breasts

waxed paper

4 ounces goat cheese

⅓ cup sun-dried tomatoes packed in oil, drained and chopped

2 tablespoons chopped fresh basil

2 tablespoons olive oil

⅓ cup chicken broth or white wine

Place the breasts one at a time between two sheets of waxed paper on a flat surface. Pound until ¼-inch thick. (You may go through several pieces of waxed paper.)

Spread 1 ounce of goat cheese on each chicken breast. Top each with 1 tablespoon sun-dried tomatoes and 1 teaspoon basil. (There will be some of each left over.) Roll up like a jellyroll and secure with toothpicks so that no filling is showing.

Heat the oil in a large skillet over medium flame and add the chicken, turning frequently until white inside and lightly browned on outside. Be sure the inside is thoroughly cooked; this takes 12–15 minutes. Remove and set aside on a warm plate. Cover with aluminum foil.

Into the Kitchen

Add the broth or wine and the remaining sun-dried tomatoes and basil. Turn up heat to high and reduce liquid by half.

Remove toothpicks from chicken and pour sauce over roll-ups. Serves 4.

Oceans of Oregano

Once you get the oregano going, there's no stopping it from spreading its tender branches several feet in all directions. By the end of the season, my husband and I just clip it back and hang it in the drying shed. When its dry, we fill old jars and give them to our nongardening friends. There's nothing finer than home made pizza dough, covered with homemade sauce and topped with homegrown oregano.

Dear common flower, that grow'st beside the way,
Fringing the dusty road with harmless gold.

—James Russell Lowell,
"To the Dandelion"

Bouquet Garni

Many recipes I make call for bouquet garni, and, before I had an herb garden, it used to drive me crazy; who has one sprig of chervil lying around? Now I just walk out to the garden and pick exactly the amount I need. If you want to use dried herbs, you can make a number of these and store in a airtight container

cheesecloth

4 sprigs fresh parsley or 1 teaspoon dried

2 sprigs fresh thyme or 1 teaspoon dried

1 bay leaf

1 sprig chervil or 1 teaspoon dried

1 sprig marjoram or 1 teaspoon dried

kitchen string

Fold the cheesecloth twice to make three layers and then cut into a 4-inch square. Place herbs onto square of cloth. Bundle up the sides and tie with string. Makes 1.

Marigold Buns

½ cup sugar

1 stick butter

2 eggs

2 cups flour

3 teaspoons baking powder

2 tablespoons apple juice

petals from 3 marigolds (also known as calendula), washed

Into the Kitchen

Preheat oven to 350°. Cream sugar and butter together in large bowl. Add eggs and beat until creamy. Sift the flour and the baking powder together and combine with sugar mixture, adding apple juice until well beaten. Stir in marigold petals.

Grease a cookie sheet and drop mixture by spoonful onto prepared sheet. Bake for 10 minutes or until lightly browned. Makes 2 dozen.

Green Tomato Pickle

Here's my grandmother's answer as to what to do with all those green tomatoes in your garden that will never turn red cause frost is coming. It can be cut down proportionately. If you have never canned anything before, be sure to read about the process in a basic cookbook like *Joy of Cooking*.

1 dry quart green tomatoes (a dry quart is $\frac{1}{6}$ larger than a liquid one, says *Joy of Cooking*)

2 large onions

$\frac{1}{3}$ cup plus 1$\frac{1}{2}$ teaspoon salt

3 cups vinegar

3 red peppers, seeded and chopped

3 green peppers, seeded and chopped

3 cloves garlic, chopped not pressed

1$\frac{1}{2}$ teaspoons dry mustard

1$\frac{1}{2}$ teaspoons whole cloves

1 tablespoon ground ginger

1$\frac{1}{2}$ teaspoons celery seed

Slice green tomatoes and onions thinly. Sprinkle with ½ cup of salt and let stand overnight. Rinse and drain.

Boil the vinegar and add the peppers and garlic and boil vigorously for 1 minute. Add the tomatoes, onions, and remaining ingredients and simmer slowly for 20 minutes. Pack while hot into hot, sterilized canning jars and seal immediately with hot, sterilized caps. Process in hot-water bath 5 minutes. Makes about 5–6 pints.

Confetti Corn Chowder

Here's a delicious chowder for those cool, early fall evenings at the end of the corn season.

1 red pepper, diced

6 cups chicken broth

kernels from 8 ears of corn

1 russet potato, peeled and cubed

1 quart low-fat milk

¼ pound bacon, fat trimmed, cut into ¼-inch pieces

1 large onion, diced

1 medium zucchini, diced

salt and pepper to taste

5 tablespoons chopped fresh parsley

2 tablespoons chopped fresh dill

½ cup slivered fresh basil leaves

Into the Kitchen

Blanch the bell pepper in boiling water for 1 minute. Drain and set aside.

Place chicken broth in large soup pot, and add half the corn and, the potato. Bring to a boil, reduce heat to medium, cover and cook until potatoes are tender, 10–15 minutes. Let cool slightly. Puree in batches, in a blender or processor, until just smooth. Transfer to a large bowl and stir in milk.

Saute bacon in the soup pot over low heat just until fat renders out, about 5 minutes. Add onion and cook until wilted, about 10 minutes. Add reserved puree, zucchini, and remaining corn kernels. Season with salt and pepper and cook for 5–8 minutes (do not boil.) Stir in blanched bell pepper and all herbs. Serves 6.

Homegrown Celery

I am addicted to growing celery. Unlike onions or broccoli, celery is a completely different creature than the store-bought variety. It is deep green and the flavor is five times as strong as its pale cousin. I love to pick a few stalks at a time instead of having to buy the whole plant and then letting it rot in the bin.

Celery Salad

This is modified from an old Shaker recipe.

3 cups sliced celery

¼ cup olive oil

¼ cup cider vinegar

½ teaspoon sugar

salt and pepper to taste

1 teaspoon chopped chives

1 tablespoon capers

Bring a pot of water to boil and add the celery. Cook until tender, about 2–3 minutes. Drain and place celery in a bowl. In a small bowl, combine the oil, vinegar, sugar, and salt and pepper and pour over the celery while still warm. Chill. Just before serving, add the chives and capers. Serves 6.

A Thorny Pleasure

We have a scramble of blackberry bushes along our side-yard fence that are volunteers from the streets' edge around our neighborhood. They are a painful problem—nothing can kill them, at least nothing I am willing to use—that I have mostly ignored, but as summer waned into fall, I decided to stop resisting and start enjoying the inevitable. So my husband and I got out containers and went blackberry picking around our neighborhood. Naturally we ate a fair number, but we ended up with enough for about a dozen jars of jam. I've been surprised at how much pleasure each jar has brought me—my very own, home-made jam.

Into the Kitchen

Blackberry Jam

This works equally well with any berries. Quantity depends on how many berries you've picked. Sometimes this comes out a bit runny; so if you're nervous, use pectin and follow the directions on the box.

hulled and washed berries

sugar

Weigh the berries and then weigh out an equal amount of sugar. Mash berries, place in a non-aluminum pan and slowly bring to a boil, stirring often. Add sugar and simmer until thick, stirring often so bottom doesn't burn. Pour into clean hot jars with sealing lids and process in a hot-water bath (see a general cookbook if you don't know how to do this) for 5 minutes.

A morning glory at my window satisfies me more than the metaphysics of books.

—Walt Whitman

Instant Gourmet

Make your own flavored olive oils, preferably from your very own garden crops. Buy some decorative bottles or use recycled wine bottles. These make fabulous gifts.

To maximize success, be sure to use only fresh herbs, wash them well, make sure the oil completely covers all the ingredients, seal the bottle tightly and use within three weeks.

Because garlic contains the spores for a bacteria that, when added to oil, can cause botulism, it's best not to make any garlic-flavored oil (the store-bought kind has sterilized the garlic.) To make chili oil, simply add 5 yellow Thai chilies and 1 teaspoon peppercorns to 5 cups of olive oil, cap the bottle tightly, and let in stand in a cool place for a week. For lemon pepper oil, slice a lemon for each bottle you plan to make and dry in oven at 170° for about 5 hours, or until dry but not crispy. To a bottle of oil, add 1 tablespoon whole black peppercorns and the slices from one dried lemon. For rosemary oil, add 3 large sprigs of rosemary to a bottle of olive oil.

Homemade Infused Vinegars

*B*efore the herbs die back in your garden, why not use them to make homemade vinegars? Packaged in pretty bottles, they make a unique gift. Pick and wash the herbs to be used (long sprigs of basil, rosemary, thyme, sage, or a combination all work well and look beautiful in the bottles). Dried herbs will not work as well. The rule of thumb is 1 cup of fresh herbs per quart of vinegar. Dry them well on paper towels. Pack the herbs

Into the Kitchen

into clean bottles or jars with lids or corks and fill with white wine vinegar that has been heated to a pre-boil. Cork or cap. Stand the jars on a sunny windowsill for about two weeks (four weeks if not very sunny). The warmth of the sun will infuse the vinegar with the herbs. Taste test; if it doesn't seem flavorful enough, strain vinegar and add more herbs. When it suits you, label and decorate the jars with a beautiful ribbon. Store at room temperature.

For a more lively infusion, try chile garlic vinegar: as many dried whole red chilies as will fit in your bottle, a tablespoon slightly crushed whole peppercorns, and five slightly crushed garlic cloves. For lemon garlic vinegar, slice up a whole lemon thinly and place in bottle with five whole slightly crushed garlic cloves and a few sprigs of thyme. Again, fill the bottles and pour the heated white wine vinegar in and cap.

Garlic Spread

This is really a confit. Slather it on sourdough baguettes or anytime a recipe calls for cooked garlic. And don't forget to use the leftover garlic-infused oil. If you have a large garlic crop or make a trip to the farmers' market, you can package this up in gift jars for friends as well as yourself.

8 ounces garlic cloves, peeled

2 cups olive oil

sterilized jars with lids that seal

In a medium saucepan, place the garlic and oil. Bring to simmer and cook over low heat for 25–30 minutes or until garlic is very tender. Cool and pack into containers. Store in refrigerator and use within two weeks. Makes 2 pounds.

Homemade Herbal Teas

It's easy to grow and make your own herbal teas, according to the folks at Yamagami's Nursery in Cupertino, California, who write that one way to start is to grow lemon verbena, lemon-grass, spearmint, and peppermint. Lemon verbena is easy to grow in full sun to part shade. Prune frequently to keep it bushy. Widely used in Asian cuisine, lemon-grass is a very fragrant clump grass that grows two to three inches tall. It likes full sun. Spearmint and peppermint like moist semi-shady areas; prune frequently to keep low, and beware—they can be invasive so you might want to grow these two in containers.

You can throw a small handful of any or all of these fresh herbs into black tea before steeping—just be sure to wash them well beforehand. Or you can dry them and experiment with a variety of combinations and additions, including carefully washed rose petals and hips, chamomile buds or leaves, or lemon or orange slices. A good basic caffeine-free recipe is 3 tablespoons dried lemon verbena, 4 tablespoons dried lemon grass, 1 tablespoon dried spearmint, and 1 tablespoon dried peppermint. Simply crumble dried herbs together, steep in 4

Into the Kitchen

cups of boiling water for 5 minutes and strain. Delicious either hot or iced.

Basil, Mint, and Rose Hip Tea

12 ounces water

2 tablespoons chopped fresh spearmint

2 tablespoons chopped fresh basil

2 rose hip tea bags

honey or sugar to taste (optional)

Place the water, spearmint, and basil in a nonreactive pan. Cover and bring the water to a rolling boil. Remove lid, stir, then add the tea bags. Steep, covered, for 3 minutes. Strain tea into 2 warmed cups. Sweeten with honey or sugar, if desired. Serves 2.

Give Your Plants a Cup of Tea

Don't throw leftover herbal tea away—use it to water your houseplants. But be sure it is caffeine-free; plants like tea as long as it is unleaded.

Pickled Crab Apples

You can use homegrown or store-bought crab apples for this.

1 quart apple cider vinegar

3 pounds brown sugar

1 tablespoon whole cloves

1 stick cinnamon

1 teaspoon ginger

1 teaspoon nutmeg

2 gallons crab apples, washed, blossom ends and stems removed

Bring all ingredients except apples to a boil. Add apples and cook until apples are tender but not mushy, about 10–15 minutes, depending on size. Remove apples, place them in sterilized jars and pour syrup over. Seal. Makes about 2 gallons.

Lavender Kisses

1 cup granulated sugar

¼ cup dried lavender flowers

1½ cups confectioners' sugar

6 egg whites, at room temperature

Cool Whip or whipped cream, optional

Preheat oven to 225°. Combine the granulated sugar and the lavender in a food processor until pulverized. Sift into a bowl with the confectioners' sugar. In a large bowl, beat egg whites with an electric mixer until soft peaks form, then gradually add the sugar mixture, beating until stiff peaks form.

Into the Kitchen

Place a sheet of aluminum foil over a cookie sheet and drop mixture by spoonfuls onto sheet an inch apart. Flatten out a bit, and bake about two hours. Kisses should be crisp but still pastel blue. Cool. Eat as is or sandwich 2 together with Cool Whip or whipped cream. Makes 3 dozen.

Thanksgiving Pumpkin Muffins

You don't have to grow your own pumpkins for these, but if you do, follow a basic recipe for cooking mashed pumpkin and then proceed.

1 large egg

$\frac{1}{2}$ cup melted butter

$\frac{1}{2}$ cup milk

1 cup canned pumpkin

$1\frac{3}{4}$ cup all-purpose flour

1 cup packed brown sugar

1 teaspoon baking soda

1 teaspoon ground ginger

1 teaspoon cinnamon

$\frac{1}{4}$ teaspoon nutmeg

$\frac{1}{4}$ teaspoon salt

Ginger Crunch Topping

$\frac{1}{2}$ cup all-purpose flour

$\frac{1}{4}$ cup brown sugar

$\frac{1}{4}$ cup finely chopped candied ginger

$\frac{1}{4}$ cup butter

To make the muffins: Break egg into a bowl and whisk in the melted butter and milk. Add pumpkin and whisk until blended. Stir in flour, brown sugar, baking soda, ginger, cinnamon, nutmeg, and salt into butter mixture. Stir until just blended. Divide batter between 12 paper-lined muffin tins.

To make the topping: Using a fork, mix together flour, brown sugar, candied ginger, and butter until crumbly. Sprinkle evenly over the tops of the muffins. Bake at 350° until cake tester inserted into the center comes out clean, about 25 minutes. Makes 1 dozen.

Pumpkin Sage Soup

    2 teaspoons olive oil

    2 large onions, chopped

    3 pounds pumpkin, seeded, peeled, and diced, or 1 large
    container canned pumpkin

    3 garlic cloves, peeled and chopped

    1 cup cooked rice

    1 teaspoon fresh sage, minced

    2 teaspoons salt (to taste)

    1 teaspoon ground white pepper

    4 cups water, approximately

    minced parsley

Into the Kitchen

Heat olive oil in a large heavy stock pot. Add onions and cook about 5 minutes on medium/high heat. Add raw pumpkin and garlic; cook for 30 minutes, stirring frequently until pumpkin is tender. (If you are using cooked pumpkin, add with the water and rice). Add water, rice, sage, salt, and pepper. Stir well and cook for 10 minutes to meld the flavors. Puree the soup in a food processor. Check the seasoning and consistency. Add more water if necessary. Garnish with minced parsley. Serve piping hot. Serves 6.

Cranberry-Pear Relish

Here's a tasty variation on the old Thanksgiving standby: cranberry sauce. It never fails to win raves when I make it. Don't be afraid of the jalapenos; it just gives it a zing.

1 tablespoon vegetable oil

½ onion, diced

1½ tablespoons minced ginger

2 garlic cloves, minced

1 large jalapeno, minced

⅓ cup red wine

⅓ cup vinegar

1 cup brown sugar

1 teaspoon pepper

1 teaspoon cinnamon

½ teaspoon allspice, ground cloves, ground coriander, and ground nutmeg

½ teaspoon dried thyme

3 cups fresh cranberries

3 pears, peeled and diced

½ cup raisins

¼ cup maple syrup

In a large saucepan, heat the oil and add the onion, ginger, garlic, and jalepeno. Cook, stirring, over medium heat until onion is tender, about 5 minutes. Add the wine, vinegar, brown sugar, and spices, and simmer, stirring occasionally, until syrupy, about 20 minutes.

Add remaining ingredients and simmer until cranberries are cooked, about 10 minutes. Serve at room temperature. Serves 6.

Into the Kitchen

Beautifying Your Home

*Natural objects themselves, even when they
make no claim to beauty, excite the feelings, and
occupy the imagination. Nature pleases, attracts,
delights, merely because it is nature. We recognize in it an Infinite Power.*

—Karl Wilhelm Humboldt

Weed Arranging

You don't need a flower garden to create beautiful arrangements. All you need is access to a field and a bit of imagination. Wild Queen Anne's lace, bittersweet, winter cress, sea
grape leaves, chive flowers, wild mustard, thistles, horsetails,
and goldenrod all look wonderful in a simple vase, either all one
variety or a combination. Even the simplicity of dried grasses or
bare willow branches can be beautiful, while various seed pods,
when dried, can make extraordinary decorations.

*Beautifying Your
Home*

*My heart and I lie small upon the earth like a
grain of throbbing sand.*

—Zitkala-Sa

Potted Candle

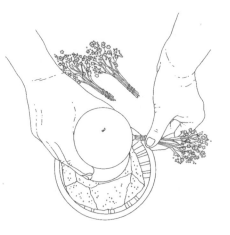

bendable dry floral foam

6-inch terra-cotta pot

4-inch diameter candle

floral wire

solidago

lavender

larskspur

miniature roses

moss

Take the floral foam and cut a piece to fit inside the pot with about 3 inches of foam above the rim. Cut off the top 4 corners at a 45° angle. Push the foam down into the pot and then push the candle into the foam.

Make 8 small bunches each of solidago and lavender, and wire each bunch with floral wire. Beginning with the solidago, push the bunches into the foam on opposite sides to maintain a balance. The lavender bunches go in next in the spaces between the solidago. Move higher and lower as you go to create a thick ring of material.

Make several small, shorter bunches each of larkspur and roses and add them randomly, filling all small gaps. Rotate the pot as you work to notice how the flowers look from different angles.

When you are satisfied with the arrangement of the flowers, take some moss and place it around the base of the candle to cover the foam.

Harvesting Herbs

*F*all is the time to harvest the herbs you've been growing all summer for wreaths, potpourri, and other flower crafts. The best time to harvest herbs is a sunny morning after the dew has evaporated. Be sure to pick at their peak—and only the amount you can dry at once.

To dry herbs in bunches, start with long-stemmed herbs like mint, artemisia, yarrow, and goldenrod. Gather into small bunches, tie the ends with string, and hang upside down in a cool, dark place, like the attic or basement or garage, and far enough apart so the air will circulate around them. An old rake head or even a clothes hanger will do. Sun or bright light will bleach out the color. If you hang them in the kitchen, be sure to keep them out of range of the sink and stove where moisture will prevent them from drying. To dry petals and leaves, scatter in a single layer on a drying tray or window screen and place where air can circulate freely around them. Leave for two to ten days; they are ready when leaves are brittle. Or if space and time are a consideration, try the microwave method.

Beautifying Your Home

Microwave Herb Drying

You easily can dry and preserve your own herbs at home, either those you've grown yourself or store-bought ones. Rinse freshly picked leaves (remove the stems) and air dry. Spread 2 cups of leaves in a single layer on a bed of paper towels in the microwave. Microwave on high for 4–6 minutes (drying time will vary according to the machine, so monitor carefully!). Cool the leaves completely before storing in an air-tight container out of direct sunlight.

> *One day with life and heart*
> *Is more than time enough to find a world.*
>
> —James Russell Lowell

Simple Wreaths

You can easily make any kind of wreath—bay leaf, evergreen, dried flower, etc., once you learn the basic technique:

1. Buy a glue gun, florist wire, and a wire-ring frame in the size you want from a floral supply store. (Take into account that the finished wreath will be several inches larger than the frame).

2. Decide on your base herb. Make sure it is long stemmed, already dried in small bunches, and that you have enough to cover the frame. Lavender, thyme, santolina, and silver king artemesia are all good. The rest of your choices will be accents. Be sure to gently handle the herbs and flowers; they are fragile.

3. Spread the bunches of herbs over the frame so that it is completely covered, overlapping in the same direction so that the stem of the previous bunch doesn't show, and attach to the frame with florist wire. This becomes your base.

4. Take smaller pieces of the same base material and tuck them around the inner and outer edges, with sprigs all going in the same direction until it is filled in in the shape you want.

5. Now take your accent flowers and place them onto the front of the base in a pleasing arrangement. Yarrow, lavender, goldenrod, and statice are good for a basic dried flower wreath; chives, marjoram, mint, and sage work well for a culinary herb wreath. Once they are in the right place, glue them with a glue gun. You can also attach cinnamon sticks, garlic bulbs, etc., by wiring them to floral picks and then sticking them into the wreath.

Beautifying Your Home

A Bay Ritual

After the first rains of November, when all the leaves are rinsed of dust, the laurel bays begin to flower in small clusters. This is the time I get ready for my holiday bay-leaf wreath making. In my own kitchen, I have used the same 10-inch steel ring for years. Before making a new wreath, I unwind the old wire and make a ritual burning of last year's leaves in the fireplace. Though the leaves are brittle, they still spark with the heavy oils that remain. Then it's time to gather a couple big bags of clipped branches with the freshest, cleanest leaves. (I suggest you do this phase outside on a picnic table since the smell of fresh bay leaves can be overwhelming. Plus, this outdoor processing gives the spiders a chance to find new homes). Then simply wind thin-gauged wire around a few branches at a time as you attach them to the heavy wire ring. For a week or two you may cry every time you enter the kitchen. This may be because you are affected by holiday sentiments or it may mean you are very sensitive to the intense oils vaporizing from your year's supply of bay leaves hanging over your oven.

I can enjoy flowers quite happily without translating them into Latin.

—Cornelia Otis Skinner

Pressed Flowers

M aking pressed flowers is incredibly easy. It requires no special equipment and costs absolutely nothing. Here's how: When your new telephone book comes, save the old one and put it somewhere where you won't lose it. Find a meadow and collect small bouquets of wildflowers. Lay them flat in different parts of the phone book. Place a small boulder, or anything else that's heavy and not likely to take off, on top of the phone book. Let sit for a few months.

> *The kiss of sun for pardon,*
> *The song of the birds for mirth—*
> *One is nearer God's Heart in a garden*
> *Than anywhere else on earth.*
>
> —Dorothy Gurney

Personalized Napkin Rings

A t the craft store, buy a set of clear Lucite napkin rings (the kind with an opening that allows you to put a piece of paper inside). Cut paper to fit inside the rings. Glue pressed flowers in any pleasing arrangement onto the paper, and cover the paper with clear, heavy tape, like that used for sending

Beautifying Your Home

packages. Insert the paper into the rings. If you can't find Lucite napkin rings, you can glue pressed flowers directly onto wooden rings, then give them several coats of shellac.

Greeting Cards

*P*lace pressed flowers in a pattern you like on the front of blank cards or on stiff artists' paper you can get at a craft or variety store. Attach them to the paper with a dab of glue. Peel an appropriate amount of transparent, self-stick plastic film (like contact paper) from the roll and carefully place on top of the flowers, pressing from the center to the edge to eliminate air bubbles. Trim the edge of the plastic to match the card or paper. You can then send them to your friends for Christmas, birthdays, Valentine's Day, or no reason at all. Bookmarks can be made in exactly the same way—just cut the paper to an appropriate size.

My garden, with its silence and pulses of fragrance that come and go on the airy undulations, affects me like sweet music. Care stops at the gates, and gazes at me wistfully through the bars.

—Alexander Smith

Pressed-Flower Paperweights

*T*hese are truly a simple pleasure. After your pressed flowers are ready, buy a hollow glass mold at a craft store. Trace the bottom of the mold onto a piece of mat board. Cut out the mat, arrange the pressed flowers on it, then glue flowers in place. Hot glue the glass mold to the mat; when dry, glue a circle of felt to the bottom.

Dried Flower Basket

*I*f you are just starting to create craft pieces for your home, try this easy idea. One advantage for beginners is that you can take the flowers out as many times as necessary to get the right look.

chicken wire

medium-sized wicker basket

amaranthus

a variety of other tall, relatively straight dried flowers (larkspur, roses, and lavender are all good)

Take the chicken wire and cut it into a circle 2 to 3 times the size of the basket opening. Form it into a flattened ball slightly larger than the basket opening and place it in the basket, filling up the whole inside.

Beautifying Your Home

Take the amaranthus and place enough of this plant into the basket to hide most of the top of the wire, but still leave room for the other flowers. (Make sure the stems go to the bottom).

Place the other flowers into the basket one type at a time. Balance the placement as you go so that when the arrangement is finished, no one type is bunched together.

Take the basket to the place it will be in your home and look at it from all angles. (This piece is particularly nice on the floor by the fireplace, but any low bench or shelf will do too). Notice how the flowers are balanced and make any adjustments that seem necessary.

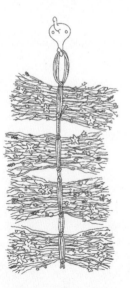

Fragrant Fires

You can bundle up mini-logs of assorted dried flowers to add fragrance to fires. Simply gather up an assortment of dried flowers and herbs still on the stems. Make into bunches about eight inches long and as big around as your fist. Tie each bundle with brown jute or raffia. When your fire is smoldering, tip with a flower log and enjoy the fragrance.

To make a hearth decoration, tie 4 or 5 bundles in a row and cut the stems down all to same length. Take a length of jute 3 times as long as you want the finished hanging to be. Fold jute in half. Place one bundle in the fold. Grasp both sides of the twine and securely tie the bundle with do a simple overhand knot Move 2 inches up the jute and tie another simple knot. This becomes bottom point for next bundle. Again tie the bundle. Continue until you've used all the bundles. You should have 12 inches or so of jute left at top. Fold that down in half and securely tie to topmost knot. This becomes the hanger.

Dried Flower Swag

dried greens such as eucalyptus, rye, or other grasses

dried flowers such as strawflowers, baby's breath, geranium, etc.

floral wire

wire cutters

glue gun

3 feet of 3-inch wired ribbon

Beautifying Your Home

Take the dried greens and create two bunches—the more, the bigger the swag. Intermingle the stems of the two bunches to create what looks like a bow tie. Wrap this in the center several times with the floral wire until it is fairly secure. Take the glue gun and squirt glue into the center to help hold the bundle together.

Take the dried flowers and wire and glue onto the swag one type at a time. Balance the types as you go and glue only at the center 3 inches. When you have put on as many types as you want, wrap the center with three or four turns of wire. Twist the ends together and cut off the excess. Wrap over this with the ribbon, hiding the wire and glue and trim to desired length. (If you want a more rustic look, use up to two dozen or so strands of raffia). Create a wire hanger in the back by wrapping floral wire, on the back side of the swag, through and around the ribbon and wire, creating a loop. Hang from wire in the back.

Nourishing Body and Soul

When the world wearies, and society ceases to satisfy, there is always the garden.

—Minnie Aumonier

Back to Basics

*I*t is early fall, and I stand surveying the wonderful harvest of tomatoes, cucumbers, string beans, Swiss chard, onions, zucchini and garlic that I grew single-handedly. As a man who grew up in the slums of Boston, the ability to grow food on my own land has always been deeply meaningful to me. This bounty, however, is not what gives me the most gratifying moment in my garden. It is what I hold in my hand. As I fondle it, I hear a ghostly standing ovation from hundreds of Irish ancestors who had starved or fled to the land of the living for what I hold here. A potato.

Nourshing Body & Soul

Skin Remedies

*Y*ou can grow and harvest a variety of herbs that will beautify and balance your skin in the bath, as well as release a variety of aromas that have various aromatherapy effects. Simply dry the herbs during the fall, and then place in a cheese cloth or muslin bag, tie it off, and drop into a tub of warm water. If you don't want to grow your own, you can order all of these plus hundreds of other herbs, muslin bags, aromatherapy oils, and books on herbs from Indiana Botanic Gardens (800-644-8327). Here's some common herbs and their suggested uses for different skin types:

> Dry, sensitive skin: borage, comfrey elder flower
>
> Mature skin: chamomile, gingko, horsetail, lavender
>
> Oily, blemished skin: calendula, echinacea, goldenseal, myrrh, sage, yarrow

Nature's Garden Facial Scrub
(for medium to dry skin)

> 1 medium-sized banana
>
> 6 strawberries, hulled
>
> 2 egg whites
>
> 2 tablespoons nonfat yogurt

Blend ingredients on high for 3–5 minutes. Apply to damp skin, and leave for 10–15 minutes.

Sandwich Mask

- ½ cup mayonnaise
- 1 large tomato
- 1 medium-sized cucumber, chopped
- ½ large avocado, mashed

Puree the ingredients in a blender or mixer until smooth. Apply to skin and allow to dry. Rinse well and follow with a light toner and moisturizer.

Inner Peace

*W*orking in the garden gives me a profound feeling of inner peace. Nothing here is in a hurry. There is no rush toward accomplishment, no blowing of trumpets. Here is the great mystery of life and growth. Everything is changing, growing, aiming at something, but silently, unboastfully, taking its time.

A Seng Song Pot of Possibilities

*T*oday on the way to our roasted-eggplant-with-provolone and-watercress yuppie lunch, my friend Jane and I drove

Nourishing Body & Soul

past a chain-link fence. It was guarding a stretch of newly turned black dirt where a Chinese woman was on her knees planting flowers. A few feet to her left, concentrating intently on the spade in his hands, was her young black-haired son. Behind them we noticed rows of huge, glazed garden pots, green, blue and black. Jane pulled over, and we decided to get out. I chose a green pot, one of the smaller ones and still nearly two feet across, crackly and with areas streaked black.

I wrote a twenty dollar check to Seng Song Pottery, admiring even the pot's flaws, including a small triangle of concrete glazed onto its side. We hauled the pot with muddy water rolling in the bottom into the back seat of Jane's car and went to lunch.

Now as I drive past rolling, grey hills toward home, just out of sight of the bay, 3:42 P.M. on I-80 by Lagoon Valley and Peña Adobe Roads near Vacaville, the pot sits empty, full of possibility, waiting to be filled with a small lemon tree, or heather, or clumps of lilies and ranunculus or even kindling and firewood if I place it by the fireplace in the house. Maybe I won't put anything in it. What I think attracted me most to these huge pots was their dark, open emptiness, waiting to receive something.

Now my green pot is propped just behind my seat. I can reach back and feel the cool glaze gritty from the nursery as I bring it home, a Seng Song pot of possibilities, like a poem— empty and full as I am.

Peppermint's Healing Qualities

*P*eppermint is one of the easiest things to grow and now it turns out that it is good for you too. Studies in Europe have shown that peppermint reduces nasal membrane inflammation, making your stuffy nose feel better. Peppermint oil also helps relieve intestinal gas and motion sickness. But according to researchers at Purdue University, there is not enough oil in commercial peppermint teas to get this effect. The good news is that it is easy to make yourself. Just harvest a big batch and allow to dry in the sun. Then store until needed. When you're feeling lowly, crush enough to make 2 teaspoons of crushed leaves, place in a tea strainer and pour a cup of boiling water over the leaves. Cover and steep for 10 minutes.

Steaming Clean

*Y*ou don't need to go to a spa or buy any fancy equipment to enjoy a facial steam. All you need is a large pot of boiling water, a sturdy table, a handful of herbs, and a bath towel. Bring a large pot of water to a boil. Remove from heat and add a handful each of whole sage leaves, whole peppermint leaves, and chamomile flowers. Carry the pot over to the table along with the bath towel and sit down in front of the pot. Drape

Nourishing Body & Soul

the towel over your head and shoulders so that you and the pot are under the towel, being sure to keep your face at least a foot away from the pot. Breath slowly and deeply through the nose, lifting the towel to get fresh air as needed. Stay under the towel tent for 5–10 minutes. Moisturize your face with a good lotion. This is not recommended if you have extremely dry skin or have heart troubles, asthma, or other trouble breathing.

Steaming Tea Facial

> 1 chamomile tea bag
>
> 1 peppermint tea bag
>
> 3 cups boiling water

Place the tea bags in a large, wide-mouthed bowl or pot. Add boiling water, and allow to cool for 2 minutes. Place a clean towel over your head and the bowl (keep your face at least eight inches away from the surface of the water), and steam for 10 minutes.

A White Paper Garden

I should like to have a grass garden. Think of the possibilities of a stretch of ground given over to it and to whatever else the wind cared to add to it by way of seedlings. The gentle little silvery grass should be there; the artistic blue grass— the tall, soldierly timothy, with its purple-fringed banners; the redtop in which one sees a forecast of oak woods in autumn; the foxtails; the quaking grasses; and many another whose names I do not know, but of whose beauties I am sure. To be perfect, this garden would slope downward to a marshy hollow, where wild rice and many sedges would grow, and should rise to a hillcrest down which winds should race over billowing, golden wheat, or grey-green oats. Maize would be planted in a field so close at hand that all summer would be filled with the music of its leaves, whisper, whisper, whispering; and somewhere about should be a patch of broom corn and of sorghum to show how regal are the growths of these largest grasses of the temperate zone.

Nourshing Body & Soul

Winter

*Every gardener knows that under the cloak of
winter lies a miracle... a seed waiting to sprout,
a bulb opening to the light, a bud straining to unfurl.
And the anticipation nurtures our dream.*

—Barbara Winkler

In the Garden

*There are two seasonal diversions that can ease
the bite of any winter. One is the January thaw.
The other is the seed catalogues.*

—Hal Borland

Keeping Track

I started a garden notebook two years ago on the suggestion of my gardening friend, Dr. Bill. We get together in the winter to do an annual seed talk and trade. We talk about our previous season's successes and failures (he lives in southern California and I in northern), ideas about watering certain plants, and what seeds we have to offer each other. I've never had a good memory and in one or two instances, when Dr. Bill asked about a certain seed I had brought along, I had no recollection of the quality of its vegetables or flowers. It was then that he pulled his gardening notebook off a shelf. It was a blank book, one of those that can be bought just about anywhere for virtually pennies, that he had decorated with a sketch of his garden.

In the Garden

What a joy to behold. Each season had a list of the dates he had planted, what he had sown, and, as the plant matured, its watering requirements and the results.

Since then I have created my own notebook and have tracked my vegetable garden. On one large page, I draw my seed-starting tray squares and list every seed I am trying to start. Once they sprout and are ready to be planted in the garden, I draw a rectangle and draw out on a page where I want things to go. This has come in very handy. I tend to buy exotic tomatoes and if I didn't have this way of keeping track, I would never know what some of them were. I used to use little plant identification sticks, but the names always faded in the sun. This way I keep track of the ones I liked (and those I didn't), so I know which seeds to plant next year. And when gardening friends come to visit, even in the dead of winter, I have my book for conversation.

I have grown wise, after many years of gardening, and no longer order recklessly from wildly alluring descriptions which make every annual sound easy to grow and as brilliant as a film star. I now know that gardening is not like that.

—Vita Sackville-West

A Garden Journal

You don't have to limit yourself to just the facts in your garden journal—it can also be a place to muse, collect quotes, and keep in touch with nature's wisdom. The key is to recognize that it can be a visual record as well as a written one—dry and paste the first sweet pea your son grew; the photos of your orchid cactus in bloom; a smattering of fall leaves on the day you found out you were pregnant surrounding by the poem your husband wrote on the occasion; sketch the color of the sky on a memorable winter day. Workshop leader Barry Hopkins, who calls these Earthbound Journals, suggests you start with a blank, hardcover artist sketchbook, at least 7½ x 8½, to allow room to paste things in, an X-acto knife for cutting, watercolors for borders, Craypas for flowers, etc., aerosol glue for pasting, and fixative to keep pencils and Craypas from smudging.

It's important that you make your own cover for the Garden Journal—you can use old bits of a special shirt, for example. If you have an electric drill, you can drill through the book to create a ribbon or rawhide fastener. The point is to follow your own creativity to where it leads you and to imbue the book with the memories of the garden.

In the Garden

Help for Neophytes

Planning a garden for first-timers can be overwhelming; it's hard to know what plants go where and, without such knowledge, you can end up with roses languishing in deep shade and tall flowers blocking the view to shorter ones. You can read a book, but sometimes too much advice can be overwhelming when you are just beginning. Garden Wheels to the rescue. These are inexpensive colorful plastic discs that rotate to show you when certain plants bloom and how different plants will work together. They come in three types: perennials, herbs and annuals. To order, call (800-723-8992).

> *To see a hillside white with dogwood bloom is to know a particular ecstasy of beauty, but to walk the gray Winter woods and find the buds which will resurrect that beauty in another May is to partake of continuity.*
>
> —Hal Borland

The Delights of Fantasy

Winter can be hard on gardening fanatics, forced indoors to attend only to the houseplants. So I always cheer myself up by collecting all the bulb and seed catalogs that come throughout the year and saving them for a dreary January weekend. I sit down at the kitchen table with them all spread out in front of me. First I pore over the beautiful color pictures and the accompanying descriptions, fantasizing about the incredible garden I could have if money, time, and weather conditions were no object: Shirley tulips "ivory white with purply pictee edge," a one-of-a-kind Batik Iris that has "dramatic white spatters and streaks against a royal purple ground," alboplenum, "doubly rare for being both multi-petaled and white."

After I have completely satisfied my eyes, I get real. I make a map of my vegetable and flower gardens, check out what seeds I have left from last year, and plot out what I want to plant. Then I go back over the catalogs again with a more selective eye and choose what I really need. Often this process goes over many days and both parts give me great pleasure: the indulging of my wildest gardening fantasies, and the anticipation of color, beauty, and form in my actual garden.

> *Nor rural sights alone, but rural sounds,*
> *Exhilarate the spirit, and restore*
> *The tone of languid nature.*

> —William Cowper

In the Garden

Great Catalogs

*G*reat, free vegetable-garden catalogs abound. Good general ones include: Park Seed (800-845-3369), The Seed Catalog (800-274-7333), and The Cook's Garden (802-824-3400). More specialized ones include: Tomato Growers Supply Company (813-768-1119), Johnny's Selected Seeds (207-437-4301) and, my personal favorite, Shepherd's Garden Seeds (in the east, 860-482-3638; in the west, 408-335-6910), which has a wide selection of unusual, easy-to-grow, disease-resistant vegetables, and lots of old-fashioned flower strains. A wonderful resource for organic gardening items including fruits, vegetables, and even weed control items, is GardensAlive! To receive a catalog, call (812-537-8650). Other good sources for organic gardeners are Harmony Farm Supply (707-823-9125, catalog costs $2) and Peaceful Valley Farm Supply (916-272-4769).

Gardener's Supply Company (800-863-1700) has wonderfully fun things for green thumbs, including kits for baking bread in terra-cotta pots, and mushroom kits. My favorite is the Vermont-Grown Kitchen Garden, which delivers an entire garden's worth of top-quality plants to your door. The set contains 71 vegetables and 27 herbs, specially selected for performance and flavor, and includes 3 each of 3 tomato varieties, 12 early and 12 late lettuces, 3 asparagus, and 9 sweet peppers. Also wonderful is White Flower Farm (800-503-9624), which carries seasonal wreaths, unique plants, and other great stuff.

Of Moon Gardens and Other Themes

Winter is the perfect time to fantasize about future gardens. A moon garden is one that has only white flowers. It's particularly striking at the moment of summer twilight when all colors except white fade and anything white takes on a luminescence that is breathtaking. That makes it a wonderful spot for evening entertaining and for those of us who work so late we only ever see our gardens in moonlight. I once went to the house of a man who was completely colorblind—any color except white or black was gray to him. He had a huge estate landscaped in beautiful, all-white beds. What stood out of course was the differences in textures and shapes: the airy froth of baby's breath combined with the dense snowballs of hydrangeas and the feathery spikes of cleomes.

For a dramatic garden design, you don't have to necessarily choose all-white. It could be all pink or all blue or all yellow. And color doesn't have to be the only theme. A friend recently told me of a garden she just saw in Colorado that was only

In the Garden

native grasses of all shapes, colors, and textures. Perhaps you are attracted to the flowers in an English cottage garden or the stylized greenery of a formal Italian garden. The point is that winter offers a great chance to imagine just what kind of outer landscape we want to create. That in itself is quite a pleasure.

> *The Snowdrop is the prophet of the flowers;*
> *It lives and dies upon its bed of snows;*
> *And like a thought of spring it comes and goes.*
>
> —George Meredith

In Winter Garb

Sometimes I think the garden is even more beautiful in its winter garb than in its gala dress of summer. I know I have thought so more than once when every leaf and branch was clothed with a pure garment of snow, so light as not to hide the grace of form. But nothing, it seems to me, could ever transcend the exquisite beauty of the vegetation when on one occasion a sharp frost followed a very wet fog. The mist driven by the wind had imparted a coating of fresh moisture, evenly distributed, over and under every leaf and twig inside the trees and shrubs as well as outside. The light coating then froze and left every innermost twig resplendent with delicate white crystals. It was quite different from an ordinary frost or a fall of snow, beautiful as are frequently the effects of these. But the glory of the scene reached its climax when the sun came out and the thicket scintillated from the center as well as its external surface.

Its dazzling splendor, however, could not last, and the glistening and enchanted spectacle gradually melted away before the greater and more glorious life-giving presence of "God's lidless eye." This gorgeous scene, however, has always dwelt in my memory and figures as the most glowing aspect a garden can assume at any season of the year.

> *I prefer winter and fall, when you feel the bone structure in the landscape—the loneliness of it—the dead feeling of winter. Something waits beneath it—the whole story doesn't show.*
>
> —Andrew Wyeth

Mad for Mushrooms?

In the Garden

Gardeners who need a fix during the cold winter months should consider a mushroom kit. They come in a number of varieties including shiitake and button. The kits contain a sterilized, enriched growing medium that is pre-inoculated with mushroom spawn that can easily be grown indoors in a cool, dark place year round. Shiitake, oyster, and portabella mushroom kits are available from Real Goods (800-762-7325), Gardener's Supply Company (800-863-1700), and Edmund Scientific Co. (609-573-6250). Edmund has a catalog with over 4000 science products including lots of other kits. Great for science-minded kids.

> *The word "miracle" aptly describes a seed.*
>
> —Jack Kramer

Brief Pleasures

*I*n the winter, some of my most powerful garden pleasures come from memory:

- That moment when you stop trying to keep your nails clean, take off your gloves, and dig wholeheartedly and carelessly into the dirt.
- Admiring that perfect rose bud with tiny dew kisses left on it, and not picking it.
- Biting into a sun-warmed, perfectly ripe strawberry.
- Eating anything you've grown in your own garden.
- Having a ladybug land on your arm.
- Showering outside after working in the yard on a hot summer day.

- The ruby and green flash of a hovering hummingbird as it feasts on the fuchsias hanging on the deck.

- Pressing your nose into a bed of moss.

- Planting flowers in someone else's garden that they won't find out about till spring.

- The smell of honeysuckle drifting in the kitchen window.

Beyond Rules

I believe in just taking my cup of coffee and clippers out to the garden in the morning and snip here and snip there. Do what you want. That way, there's never this awful feeling that the fourteenth of February is Valentine's Day and your roses must be fed promptly on Valentine's Day. People's lives are regimented enough without all that.

Seed Savers Exchange

In the Garden

*F*or more than two decades, members of the nonprofit, grassroots organization Seed Savers Exchange (SSE) have been searching the countryside for "heirloom" varieties of vegetables and fruits. Kent and Diane Whealy founded SSE in 1975, after Diane's grandfather entrusted them with garden seeds that his parents had brought from Bavaria. The Whealys began searching for other gardeners who were also keeping heirloom varieties and soon discovered a vast, little-known genetic treasure.

Today SSE's 8,000 members are working together to collect, maintain, and distribute thousands of heirloom vegetables and fruits. Last year 1,000 of SSE's members used Seed Savers Yearbook, one of three annual publications, to distribute the seeds of 11,000 rare food crops to other interested gardeners. Each year SSE's members offer twice as many varieties as are available from the entire mail-order garden-seed industry in the U.S. and Canada. Since it was founded in 1975, SSE's members have distributed an estimated 750,000 samples of heirloom seeds that are not available in catalogs and are often on the verge of extinction. If you will like to donate or receive heirloom seeds (or both), consider joining. Call (319-382-5990) or FAX (319-382-5872) to receive a free four-page brochure that describes the organization.

Winter Chores

Winter is the time for doing all those garden tasks we were too busy during the rest of the year to tackle. As you've transplanted things, chances are you've accumulated a goodly number of empty pots. Winter is when you should scrub those pots with bleach so you can use them again without taking the chance of infecting your new plants with old bugs. This is also the time to sterilize any dirt (200° F in oven for 3 hours) you might want to use for spring houseplant repotting.

> *Despite March's windy reputation, winter isn't really blown away: it is washed away. It flows down all the hills, goes swirling down the valleys and spills out to sea. Like so many of this earth's elements, winter itself is soluble in water.*
>
> —Anonymous

The Winter Garden

*T*he last handful of yellow leaves cling to the tips of the favorite apple tree—the one with the thirty-eight grafts that in the summer, shades the north court. The dawn redwood sheds its bright, rusted foliage almost overnight, making a fine fluffy blanket for the azalea bed below. The garden has started its winter sleep. But not the birds!

In the Garden

The first notes I hear these frosty AMs as I let out the dogs is, "Chit! Chit!" from the big hachiya persimmon on the hill.

Fluttering about the bare branches, white tail spots flashing, is a pair of Audubon's warblers, down from the snowy mountains and probably on their way to even warmer climes, south. They have stayed here almost three weeks, ever since a few beautiful orange persimmon fruits have ripened enough to attract flies.

Another surprise flashed past, this time in the south court, where a diminutive chickadee was pecking away at the hard fat in a wire basket. The chickadee had pecked himself a small cave that almost hid his energetic little form, as a big California thrasher, three times his size, landed on the chunk of fat with a big, curved bill poised ready to peck. Out flew the startled chickadee, darting enraged at the big brown thrasher—who flew meekly off, defeated by the midget. The chickadee returned to his suet cave. To peck in peace. (Even jays are intimidated by thrashers. What happened?)

This has been a good year for toyon berries, and all December I have enjoyed the bright sprays viewed through the sink window. Today the cedar waxwings arrived, and that signaled the end of the berries. Fair enough, I have enjoyed them, now it's the birds' turn. The news spread fast. There was only a quintet of waxwings swinging upside down to gulp (how do they swallow up hill?), but several robins, who have ignored the berries up to today, arrived to help out.

Lots happening in the winter garden!

Water Consciousness

*I*f you live in a spot where water is scarce, consider a Xeriscape. Xeriscaping (from the Greek word *xeros*, meaning dry) is a form of landscaping that uses little water—up to 60 percent less if done right. The fundamentals of such gardening include using native plants, large quantities of mulch, and more efficient irrigation systems. You don't even have to live in a thirsty part of the country to benefit from such principles. By watering less and using less chemicals wherever your garden is, you help stop ecological mayhem in your own backyard.

One way to get started is to choose plants that grow naturally within a fifty-mile radius of where you live. Water districts, native plant societies, university extension departments and even some nurseries usually keep such lists. The next is to place plants together that have like water needs. Roses next to cacti is not the way to go, but xeriscaping does allow for a limited number of water guzzlers like roses in oases that are located in highly visible places. For more information, consult your water district, university agriculture extension, or local nursery.

Who loves a garden loves a greenhouse too.

—William Cowper

In the Garden

Indoor Gardens

*I*n the winter when my garden is dry and bare, nothing gives me more pleasure than a visit to the local garden shop, where it always feels like sweet, balmy summer. I wander through the rows of brightly colored flowers and richly hued shiny leaves, and the aroma of blossoms and sweet rich earth make me forget, for a time, the gloom and doom outside. The plants and flowers are completely oblivious to the weather outside, and their verdant outbursts of energy restore my own. I take an inordinate amount of time picking out some ridiculously expensive and riotously colored plant that just screams warm weather, which I take home and place on my windowsill or bedside table in a beautiful basket or brightly colored cachepot. I have kind of a brown thumb, so my plants never last long, but I almost prefer that; it gives me a chance to go to the garden shop again that much sooner.

Topiary Tricks

*I*f you are attracted to the topiaries you see at botanical gardens, you might want to try growing one of your own. First you need a frame. Some home and garden stores are now carrying them but you can also get them from Cliff Finch Zoo

(209-822-2315); Topiaries Unlimited (802-823-5536), and Topiary Inc. (must write for catalog: 41 Bering St., Tampa FL 33606).

Then you pick a plant to cover it with. You must think about where the topiary will be—sun or shade? Is it small enough to be brought inside in winter or must the plant be winter hardy? Then you must think of the plant itself—does it shear nicely (to keep the shape you must give it a haircut regularly). Is the leaf size in proportion to the frame, and will the texture be right for your desired effect? Good topiary plants include ivy, star jasmine, purple bell vine, Japanese boxwood, pyracantha, rosemary, lavender, and compact myrtle.

> *Everything in nature invites us constantly to be what we are.*
>
> —Gretel Ehrlich

The Ultimate Mud Pie

*T*he first week of January, when the rain is pouring down in buckets, I set aside a day to get out in the garden in my rubber boots and my most disreputable clothes. This is the time of year when the compost box looks its worst—a bulging mix of leaves, twigs, weeds, flower stalks, and kitchen waste, all soggy

In the Garden

and far too cold to decay. I take the biggest fork I can lay my hands on and take the slats off the box and fork the whole mess onto the ground. Then I make separate piles of other ingredients: a dozen garbage bags of horse manure, ripe, pungent, and full of promise; a heap of sea lettuce, dragged up from the beach after the November storms; and a pile of ordinary dirt. Then comes the best part: piling it all together in layers like a really gooey Black Forest cake, except with manure instead of cherries.

By now, I'm covered in dirt and rain and bits of seaweed, and I'm sliding around in the muck and having the time of my life, though anybody else might think I was doing an unpleasant chore. Finally I cover the new compost heap up in black plastic and head indoors for the hottest bath I can stand.

And then comes the moment of greatest pleasure: the sunny day in February when I peel back the plastic and smell the rich odor of decay and see the warm steam rising. A fork plunged into the pile reveals my greatest hope come true: a mass of seething worms, working their little hearts out to turn my compost pile into rich black soil. There's no magic like it.

> *Nature: The Unseen Intelligence which loved us*
> *into being, and is disposing of us by the same*
> *token.*
>
> —Elbert Hubbard

The Pleasure of Periwinkle

*G*rowing older has shown me the value of ground covers: hale survivors they are. Ground covers do just what their name promises, at varying rates of speed. My favorite is periwinkle or vinca minor—deep evergreen foliage that vines and hugs the ground and will grow up a hill or along a wall in the poorest of soil. I placed one tiny plant alongside the chimney of my house, a place that had defied other plantsIt thrives there still and has spread over the years to cover an entire hill. A few years ago, I undertook a scholarly research project about *Gawain and the Green Knight*, the epic poem in Middle English. To my great surprise and delight, I discovered that mysterious women had embroidered periwinkle onto Gawain's cape before his heroic journey to confront the monstrous Green Knight. As I dug deeper in the arcana section of my library, I discovered that periwinkle had been made into wreaths and placed on the heads of young men going to battle in medieval England. What a rich history my favorite humble ground cover comes from!

> *In his garden every man may be his own artist without apology or explanation. Here is one spot where each may experience "the romance of possibility."*
>
> —Louise Beebe Wilder

In the Garden

With Family and Friends

*How can those who do not garden, who have
no lot in the great fraternity of those who watch
the changing years as it affects the earth and its
growth, how can they keep warm their hearts in
winter?*

—Mrs. Francis King

A Memory Garden

It all started when my father died and friends gave me a white rhododendron as a sympathy gift. I noticed that every year when it bloomed, memories of my father would come flooding back. Then my husband's mother died, and friends sent a crab apple tree. When that burst into bloom, we would think of her as well. We decided to turn that whole section of our yard into a memory garden: the early blooming azalea my daughter, who lives in California, sent me for Mother's Day; the scented geraniums my old friend Kay once gave me a slip of; the weeping cherry we planted in honor of my husband's father; the clematis that was my husband's holiday gift from his sister. Now, as the seasons turn and the plants bloom in its turn, our thoughts go

*With Family
& Friends*

out to the person the plant symbolizes, and we draw him or her close once again.

A garden is a place to feel the beauty of solitude.

—Bob Barnes

A Birth Tree

*Y*ou don't have to wait till someone dies or moves away to have a plant in their honor. My husband and I planted a hydrangea that was on the altar at our wedding. It moves with us from house to house as a symbol of our marriage. And many people have planted birth trees for their children. You can involve your child in helping take care of the tree and track its growth by tying a bit of yarn to the outmost tip of a branch each fall and see where the yarn ends up after the summer.

Stealing Beauty

*L*ong ago, ladies considered houseplants very precious. When they secured a new variety they would guard it jealously. My mother, who was sometimes a bit naughty, would carry a folded bread wrapper in her purse (plastic bags being unknown at the time) just in case she could talk someone into giving her a "slip" (as cuttings were called in those days). Once, she could not resist, when her hostess was out of the room preparing refreshments, snipping off a tiny bit of a cherished plant and slipping it into her purse. She carefully tended the cutting and it grew. Every time her friend came over I had to run out and hide it. One day she came over unexpectedly, and I remember what a dreadful time my mother had trying to explain.

> *Everybody needs beauty as well as bread, places*
> *to play in and pray in, where Nature may heal*
> *and cheer and give strength to body and soul*
> *alike.*
>
> —John Muir

Gardening Clubs

For as long as I can remember, my mother belonged to a garden club. Once a month throughout the year, she would go off somewhere, no matter where we lived. It was all very mysterious to me; what did those ladies do together? About once a year, it would be her turn to host the club, and she would

With Family
& Friends

work even more diligently in her flower beds, making them perfect. I remember tea and bearded iris in bloom.

Throughout the country, garden clubs continue to be popular, especially among the retired set. If you are interested in joining one, just ask around at your local nursery. If time during weekdays is an issue for you, consider the National Home Gardening Club. Dues are only one dollar per month and membership includes a number of unique benefits such as product-testing privileges (companies send their latest products such as mowers, rakes, and hoses, and members try them out, issue a report, and get to keep them), your garden photos and garden tips published in their how-to magazine, a directory of public gardens, free plants, and member-only product offers. If you are interested in joining, write to National Home Gardening Club, 12301 Whitewater Drive, Monnetonka, MN 55343.

He who plants a garden plants happiness.

—Chinese proverb

Gardening Gifts

Winter is the time for gift giving and there is something out there for every gardener on your list. Here is a listing of some of the best garden gift catalogs I know: Orchids, Etc., (800-525-7510), plants, fresh flowers, and floral gifts; Casual Living, (800-843-1881), great garden furniture, home and outdoor living acoutrements, Gardener's Eden, (800-822-1214), garden tools and apparel, landscaping accessories, live plants, and flowers; Mountain Farms, Inc., (704-628-4709), dried herbs and flowers; Smith & Hawken, (800-776-3336), wonderful plants and tools, fountains, outdoor furniture, pond kits, books, gardening clothes and accessories; Spring Hill Nurseries (800-582-8527), bonsai, perennials, annuals, ground covers, fruit tress, and gardening supplies; Plow & Hearth (800-627-1712), unique items such as landscape bridges, martin houses, and pond kits, as well as furniture and garden supplies; Winterthur Museum & Gardens, (800-767-0500), upscale outdoor art, jewelry, garden materials, and home decor accessories; Gardener's Supply Company, (800-863-1700), great nontoxic solutions to pesticides, composting containers, and lots of water-saving and other unique gardening supplies.

> *I'd rather have roses on my table than diamonds on my neck.*
>
> —Emma Goldman

With Family & Friends

A Blooming Card

*S*omeone figured out how to plant seeds inside paper and now there are a variety of places you can get wonderful cards and notepaper that can be written on, mailed, and then planted either inside or out by your lucky letter recipient. Some of best ones I've seen are done by the Santa Fe Farmer's Market Cooperative Store and are handmade from organic and recycled materials and studded with flowers, herbs, and vegetable seeds. The paper disintegrates when you plant it, and the seeds blossom into evidence of your feelings. Available from Seeds of Change (888-762-7333).

> *Some persons may think, that Flowers are things*
> *of no use; that they are nonsensical things. The*
> *same may be, and perhaps with more reason, said*
> *of Pictures. An Italian, while he gives his fortune*
> *for a picture, will laugh to scorn a Hollander,*
> *who leaves a tulip-root as a fortune to his son.*
> *For my part, as a thing to keep and not to sell:*
> *as a thing, the possession of which is to give me*
> *pleasure, I hesitate not a moment to prefer the*
> *plant of a fine carnation to a gold watch set with*
> *diamonds.*
>
> —William Cobbett

Faithful Ground Cover

My great aunt Ida had an intriguing plant that grew everywhere on her place in attractive clumps. It never bloomed, but I noticed that it looked nice beside other plants with its low mass of green and white variegated leaves. It seemed to make the other plants it grew near look even better. Aunt Ida, a hardy ninety years old at the time, claimed she had come to depend on it to cover unattractive well covers, eave spouts, and the like. Eventually, I came away from her house with a small clump that I put in problem areas where nothing else seemed to want to grow. I especially liked that Aunt Ida's plant couldn't be found at the nurseries I dragged my mother to every weekend. But best of all, I loved the name of Aunt Ida's faithful ground cover which conjured up images of far-off places. She called it, "Snow on the Mountain."

How doth the little busy bee
Improve each shining hour,
And gather honey all the day
From every opening flower!

—Isaac Watts

With Family
& Friends

Ornamental Pleasures

*B*oth these ornaments are so easy to make, they are perfect for young kids (if you help with the glue gun). Make lots—save some for your tree and give the rest away as presents to teachers, the mailman, grandma, etc.

Pinecone Ornaments

> small pinecones
>
> 7-inch lengths of very narrow ribbon
>
> dried rosebuds
>
> glue gun

Note: The size of the ribbon and the roses should be proportionate to the size of the cones.

Place pinecones in a paper bag. Put into the microwave and heat for 8–10 minutes. (This is to kill any bugs.) If you want the cones to open and this hasn't opened them, keep heating the same way at 3-minute intervals until they open.

Take the ribbon, fold it in half and hot-glue the ends to the stem-end of the cone. Take a bud or two and hot-glue them on top of the ribbon ends to hide them. Repeat until all cones are gone.

Citrus Ornaments

> 3–4 lemons, oranges, and/or limes
>
> gold cord
>
> various small, dried flowers and leaves
>
> berries, narrow ribbon, and other decorative items
>
> glue gun

Cut the fruit into ¼-inch slices. Place four layers of paper towels on a microwave-safe plate and arrange the citrus slices on the paper towels. (If they don't all fit in one layer, do it in batches.) Cover with another sheet of paper towel and heat at 50% power for 2 minutes. Turn the slices over and place them on dry spots. Repeat until dry. (Note: If the bottom towels become too wet during this process, replace with four new sheets.)

Cut the gold cord into 6-inch lengths, 1 piece for each slice. Fold cord in half and glue the ends together to the back of a citrus slice. Pick out various dried flowers and leaves, and bits of ribbon and other trim, and glue them to the front of the slice.

Fire Starters

With Family & Friends

A great, easy, and inexpensive gift for older kids to make for the holidays is Fire Starter Pinecones. Simply gather a quantity of dried pinecones. Melt a block of paraffin in the top of a double boiler. As it melts, add one red crayon and a few drops of cinnamon or pine essential oil. When the paraffin is completely melted and stirred, grasp a pinecone with a pair of old tongs, and tip completely in the wax. Set on a piece of waxed paper to harden. Repeat until you're done. Place hardened cones in a basket, add a ribbon, and voilà!

All my hurts
My garden spade can heal.

—Ralph Waldo Emerson

Their Own Greenhouse

*I*f you are feeling extravagant and really want to please the serious gardener in your life, consider buying a freestanding greenhouse. Sturdi-Built Greenhouse has a number of redwood and glass options in various sizes to choose from. For a catalog, call (800-722-4115).

Into the Kitchen

*Property is for the comfort of life, not for the
accumulation of wealth. A sage, having been
asked who is lucky and who is not, replied:
"He is lucky who has eaten and sowed, but he
is unlucky who has died and not enjoyed."*

—Sa'di

Spiced Red Wine with Brandy and Citrus

This is a bit different from mulled wine because it is served
at room temperature. You must start at least 3 weeks in advance.

1 orange, peeled and sliced (keep the rind)

½ lemon, sliced

1 vanilla bean

6 whole cloves

1 750-ml bottle dry red wine

½ cup framboise *eau-de-vie* (clear raspberry brandy) or other
brandy

6 tablespoons sugar

Into the Kitchen

Combine sliced orange and lemon, orange rind, vanilla
bean, and cloves in large glass jar. Pour wine over. Cover and
place in cool dark area for 2 weeks.

Strain wine through several layers of cheesecloth into 4-cup measuring cup. Discard solids. Add framboise and sugar to wine; stir until sugar dissolves. Pour mixture into wine bottle or decorative bottle. Cork and place in cool dark area for at least 1 week. Can be made 6 weeks ahead. Store in cool dark area. Makes about 1 750-ml bottle.

Lemon Geranium Sponge Cake

This old-fashioned treat can be made any time of the year.

⅓ cup honey

3 tablespoons flour

¼ cup fresh lemon juice

1 teaspoon grated lemon peel

2 eggs, separated

1 cup milk

5 drops geranium oil

rose geranium leaves, optional

Preheat oven to 325° F. Beat together honey, flour, lemon juice, and rind. Add yolks, milk, and geranium oil and mix again. In a separate bowl, beat egg whites until stiff, and fold into the lemon mixture. Pour into a buttered 8-inch-square baking pan and place in a pan of hot water. If available, lay fresh rose geranium leaves on top of the pudding. Bake for 45–50 minutes, or until cake is set and knife comes out clean. Serve warm. Serves 6.

> *The best thing to do with water is to use a lot of it.*
>
> —Philip Johnson, on
> designing fountains

Sprout Your Own

*B*ack in my commune days, I used to be in charge of making the sprouts and yogurt for the week. (With a bad back, I was exempt from the more strenuous chores.) With twenty-five people on a vegetarian diet, we went through a lot of both. To this day, twenty years later, I can't bring myself to buy sprouts from the store. It's just too easy (and satisfying) to do on your own.

Raw sprouts are a wonderful source of vitamins. Any beans—soy, fava, lima, pinto, garbanzo—can be sprouted, as can alfalfa, sunflower, peas, lentils, and many other seeds. Just be sure never to try potatoes or tomatoes—the sprouts are poisonous. And don't sprout seeds that have been sold for garden planting; they've probably been treated with a fungicide. Untreated seeds are available at health food stores. Every seed takes a slightly different amount of soaking and sprouting time.

Into the Kitchen

For complete details for various spouts plus recipes, see *Sprouting for All Seasons* by Bertha B. Larimore, published by Horizon and available by calling (801-295-9451).

> *One day, the gardener realizes that what she is doing out there is actually teaching herself to garden by performing a series of experiments.*
>
> —Margaret Roach

Alfalfa Sprouts in a Jar

    2 tablespoons alfalfa seeds
    1 wide-mouth quart jar
    water
    cheesecloth
    rubber band

Place the seeds in the bottom of the jar and fill with water. Put cheesecloth over the top and secure with a rubber band. Store in a warm, dark place like a kitchen cupboard. Two or three times a day take the jar out, empty the water and add new water. They will be ready in 4–5 days and will keep up to a week in the refrigerator. Makes 1 quart.

Spiced Almonds

For the nut lovers on your shopping list, make your own spiced nuts. Package in a beautiful tin with a pretty bow.

2 tablespoons butter

1 teaspoon cinnamon

1 teaspoon ground cumin

$\frac{1}{2}$ teaspoon ground coriander

$\frac{1}{4}$ teaspoon (or more, depending on taste) cayenne pepper

$2\frac{1}{2}$ cups raw almonds

2 tablespoons sugar

1 teaspoon salt

Preheat oven to 300° F. In a large skillet, melt the butter and add cinnamon, cumin, coriander, and cayenne. Cook, stirring constantly, about 30 seconds, until very fragrant. Add the nuts, stir to coat. Then add sugar and salt and stir again. Transfer to baking sheet and bake, stirring occasionally, until nuts are roasted, about 20 minutes. Will store up to one month if in a tightly sealed container.

Winter-Fresh Herbs

One benefit of an herb patch in your garden is that you can just pick what you need for that night's dinner: no worrying about fresh parsley or basil rotting in the bottom drawer of the fridge. But even inveterate gardeners end up having to buy herbs outside of the growing season and keeping them fresh can

Into the Kitchen

be a real struggle. If you follow a few simple tips, however, you can greatly expand their life. The trick is to treat them as you would cut flowers.

First, untie and immerse in cool water; don't run under the faucet, that can damage tender leaves. Pick through and discard any rotting stems or leaves. Shake herbs dry gently; never use a salad spinner: it's too rough. Place the bunch stems down in a vase or canning jar that allows the leaves to stay above the rim. With basil, just store on your counter top; it will keep up to a month and may even sprout roots. With all other fresh herbs, loosely cover with a plastic bag and stick in the refrigerator. Change water every few days. Chervil, chives, dill, thyme, and watercress will keep up to a week like this; cilantro and tarragon, two weeks; and parsley as long as three weeks.

Herb Bread

1 teaspoon sugar

4 cups warm water

1 tablespoon yeast

12 cups bread flour

1 tablespoon salt

3 tablespoons chopped fresh basil

2 tablespoons chopped rosemary

1 cup sun-dried tomatoes, drained and chopped

²/₃ cup olive oil

extra oil and rosemary for top

In a small bowl, combine sugar, ⅔ cup water, and yeast. Let sit in a warm spot until frothy, about 10 minutes. In a large bowl, combine the flour, salt, herbs, and tomatoes. Add the oil and yeast mixture, then gradually add the remaining warm water. As dough gets stiff, mix with your hands, until it is soft but not sticky.

Turn onto a lightly-floured surface and knead for 5 minutes. Place back in bowl, cover with a towel, and place in a warm spot until doubled in size, about 40 minutes.

Preheat oven to 425° F. Knead again until elastic, then cut into three equal pieces. Shape each into a round and arrange on oiled baking sheets. Brush a bit of oil on each loaf and top with a few rosemary leaves. Bake until golden brown and hollow sounding when tapped, about 25 minutes. Makes 3 7-inch loaves.

Provençal Potatoes

This hearty French dish is a perfect winter accompaniment to grilled or roasted meat.

Into the Kitchen

1½ pounds potatoes, sliced

4 shallots, sliced

3 garlic cloves, sliced

salt and pepper to taste

1 teaspoon chopped fresh thyme or ¼ teaspoon dried

½ cup dry white wine

⅔ cup pitted black olives such as niçoise or kalamata

Preheat oven to 375° F. Combine all ingredients in a casserole dish and bake, uncovered, until potatoes are tender and liquid is absorbed, about 30–40 minutes. Stir occasionally and add a bit of water if necessary. Serves 4.

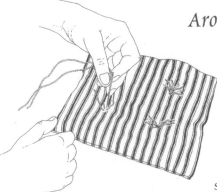

Aromatic Trivet

*T*his is a kitchen delight that will release a fabulous fragrance into the air every time you place a hot pan on it. It's so simple to do you should consider making some for yourself and for your friends.

20 inches sturdy fabric, such as mattress ticking

scissors

needle and thread

stuffing: broken cinnamon sticks, cloves, and bay leaves

upholstery needle

cotton string

Cut two 20–25 inch pieces of fabric and place right sides together. Pin and stitch the pieces together, leaving an opening large enough for the stuffing to fit through. Trim the seams and turn right-side out. Fill with stuffing material and then slip stitch the opening using the upholstery needle threaded with string. Make four separate stitches in the center of the pad, forming a square, clearing the contents away from the stitch. Finish each with a simple knot.

Makes 1 pad

Homemade Vanilla Extract

Yes, you can do it, and it is unbelievably easy. If you place it in a pretty glass bottle, it makes a lovely little gift.

1 vanilla bean

1 4-ounce bottle with top

scant 4 ounces vodka

Split the bean in half, put in the bottle, and pour in the vodka. Cap and let sit at least one month. (The longer, the stronger.)

Into the Kitchen

Mulled Cranberry Cider

Here's a twist on an old winter favorite

4 cups cider

4 cups cranberry juice

6 cloves

1 stick cinnamon

4 whole allspice

$\frac{1}{2}$ cup brown sugar

Bring all ingredients to a simmer in a large pot, stirring till sugar melts. Strain and serve. Makes 8 cups.

Summer in a Jar

*I*n February, I love to open the cabinet to look at the jars of tomato sauce I canned the previous August. The jars look like dark red jewels and when opened smell exactly like sweet summer.

I plant rosemary all over the garden, so pleasant it is now that at every few steps one may draw the kindly branchlets through one's hand, and have the enjoyment of their incomparable incense.

—Gertrude Jekyll

The Simplicity of Soup

*I*t is a wintery Sunday morning. The sun is streaming through the kitchen windows onto newly wiped counters. A stack of fresh vegetables waits on the cutting board. The beans, soaked overnight, are rinsed and in a colander, ham hocks are simmering succulently on the stove, and five gleaming white bowls stand empty by the sink. I am about to make Portuguese Bean Soup, and all is right with the world.

First the carrots, cut across, form perfect orange disks which seem to glow as they fill one of my lovely white bowls. Then the onions . . . whack, whack, whack . . . become immaculate pearly wedges glittering in a second bowl, side by side with the carrots. The orange and pearl are now joined by a bowl filled with pale green celery slices. Raw potato cubes add to the line-up and soon the fifth bowl overflows with ruffly, shredded cabbage. A mound of lacy, chopped parsley rests on the counter top. The aroma of simmering ham is soon complemented by the scent of freshly squeezed lemon juice and then by the enticing, pungent odor of minced garlic. These glorious ingredients will soon join forces to become the feast my family and I love. Surveying the colorful, aromatic, magnificent array I have created, I feel like Mother Earth, Pablo Picasso, and Johnny Appleseed rolled into one.

Into the Kitchen

Portuguese Bean Soup

½ pound dried kidney beans

2–3 ham hocks sauteed

3 carrots, sliced

1 onion, sliced

3 stalks celery, sliced

2 large baking potatoes, cut into ¾ inch cubes

3 tablespoons parsley, minced

1 tablespoon lemon juice

2 cloves garlic, minced

salt and pepper

1 8 ounce can tomato sauce

½ head cabbage, shredded

2 pounds Portuguese sausage, sliced thinly

½ cup uncooked macaroni

Soak the beans in water overnight. Simmer the ham hocks in water to cover for 1½ hours. When tender, remove, discard bones, shred meat, and set aside. Add the drained beans to the broth and cook for 1 hour. Add the carrots, onion, celery, potatoes, parsley, lemon juice, garlic, salt, pepper, and tomato sauce, and cook until the vegetables are tender. Add cabbage, sausage, and macaroni and cook until the macaroni is done. Serves 6.

Almost Home Grown

OK, so this story isn't about my own garden, but about someone else's. About six months ago, I saw an ad for organic produce, delivered weekly to your door. I called the number and decided to sign up because the price—twenty-five dollars for enough vegetables for two people for a week—sounded like no more than I pay at the grocery store (and a lot less than those fancy natural food stores). I've been delighted. The box shows up on my doorstep every Friday afternoon, and it gives me great pleasure to eat only organic foods and to help provide employment for small farmers. Eating in season, though, has taken some getting used to—in the winter there was a time when I thought if I had to eat another eggplant I was going to go nuts and right now we're suffering from an over-abundance of basil—and I still supplement occasionally by buying something I can't live without from the store. But it has made me eat things I would never have bought (spring garlic shoots are incredible!), and I find I'm eating more fruits and vegetables in general than ever before. Mostly I like the groundedness of it all—when it's spinach season, that's what you eat; when there are peaches, you can have them. And when the season is over, that's it till next year. Just another way of reminding me of the cycles of life.

Into the Kitchen

Winter Stew

A satisfying and simple light supper. Just omit the sausage and you have a vegetarian entree. Can be served over rice.

2 tablespoons olive oil

$\frac{1}{4}$ cup green or pepper

1 cup chopped onion

4 cloves chopped garlic

2 cups chopped fresh spinach

2 cups chopped cabbage

1 $14\frac{1}{2}$-ounce can tomatoes

1 cup frozen lima beans

4 ounces fully cooked sausage, such as andouille (for a spicier stew) or kielbasa, sliced

$\frac{1}{4}$ cup chopped parsley

2 $14\frac{1}{2}$-ounce cans of beef, chicken, or vegetable broth

In a large pot, heat the olive oil over medium-high heat and add green pepper, onion, and garlic. Saute until vegetables are tender, about 5 minutes. Add the remaining ingredients and simmer until cabbage is cooked, about 10 minutes. Serves 4.

Poached Fruit

When the weather turns cold, I always get a hankering for poached winter fruit. Here's one of my favorite recipes.

2 cups sugar

4 cups water

1 lemon, cut in half

2 sticks cinnamon

4 cloves

6 whole allspice

$\frac{1}{8}$ teaspoon nutmeg

3 apples, peeled and diced

3 pears, peeled and diced

1 orange, peel on and sliced crosswise into very thin slices

2 cups fresh cranberries

$\frac{1}{4}$ cup dried fruit

Combine the sugar and water in a large heavy saucepan over medium-high heat and cook until sugar is dissolved. Squeeze lemon into the pot, then add the rind. Add the spices and simmer for about 5 minutes to blend flavors. Add fruit and cook only until fruit is tender, about 5–10 minutes. Remove lemon rind and serve warm. Serves 6.

Cabbage Creativity

Winter is cabbage season and there are all kinds of delicious ways to serve this healthful head. These two recipes never fail to win me compliments.

Into the Kitchen

Curried Coleslaw

¼ cup apple cider vinegar

4 tablespoons nonfat yogurt

2 teaspoons sugar

½–1 teaspoon curry powder, depending on your taste

salt and pepper to taste

4 cups shredded cabbage

1 large carrot, shredded

½ cup green pepper, chopped

1 tablespoon minced onion

Combine vinegar, yogurt, sugar, curry powder, and salt and pepper in a small bowl. In a large bowl, combine the cabbage, carrot, green pepper, and onion. Add dressing, mix well, and chill at least 2 hours. Serves 4.

Cabbage and Leek Salad

1 tablespoon plus ½ cup olive oil

6 small leeks, cut in half lengthwise and well cleaned

1 small head of cabbage

2 cups water

4 tablespoons white wine vinegar

1 tablespoon Dijon mustard

salt and pepper to taste

In a large frying pan with a lid, heat the 1 tablespoon oil over medium heat and add the leeks. Saute for 2 minutes. Core the cabbage and cut into 6 equal pieces. Add to the leeks with the water and 3 tablespoons vinegar. Cover and simmer for 10 minutes, then uncover and simmer for 30 minutes, until vegetables are tender and most of liquid has cooked off.

While cabbage is cooking, in a small bowl, combine remaining 1 tablespoon of vinegar and the mustard. Whisk in the remaining ½ cup oil. When vegetables are done, drain off liquid and place on a serving platter. Pour dressing over and add salt and pepper to taste. Serve warm. Serves 6.

> *When I was most tired, particularly after a hot safari in the dry, dusty plains, I always found relaxation and refreshment in my garden. It was my shop window of loveliness, and Nature changed in regularly that I might feast my hungry eyes upon it. Lone female that I was, this was my special world of beauty: there were my changing styles and my fashion parade.*
>
> —Osa Johnson

Into the Kitchen

Beautifying Your Home

A house with daffodils in it is a house lit up,
whether or not the sun be shining outside.
Daffodils in a green bowl—and let it snow if
it will.

—A. A. Milne

Alternative Christmas Trees

- I have a large yard that can accommodate more trees, so every Christmas we buy a small live evergreen. We decorate it with popcorn and cranberry strands and when the holidays are over, plant it outside, complete with decorations. The birds love it!

- We decorate our live Christmas tree with tiny bouquets of dried flowers and use thin ribbon as hangers.

- We bundle cinnamon sticks together with raffia and hang them from our tree along with bundles of small pinecones and holly twigs that we wire together with garden wire.

Beautifying Your
Home

Apple Pomanders

Stud apples with whole cloves, then roll in a mixture of equal parts ground cinnamon, nutmeg, cloves, and orris root (available at herb stores and through herbal catalogs). Let dry in a warm, dry, dark place. When dry, place in a bowl to fill a room with a delightful aroma.

If Eve had had a spade and known what to do
with it, we should not have had all that sad
business about the apple.

—Elizabeth von Arnium

A Passion for Pails

An everyday, galvanized metal bucket (available at most hardware and garden stores) makes a wonderful and unique planter, gift container, or desk accessory. Coat the exterior and interior of your bucket with latex enamel spray paint and let dry (if you prefer a high gloss, you may want to add a coat of clear lacquer). If you will be growing live plants in your bucket, don't forget to drill a small drainage hole in the bottom of the pail.

Holiday Centerpiece

*T*his beautiful table arrangement of candles and greens couldn't be simpler to make; just be sure to use dripless candles.

  shallow waterproof bowl

  large circular plate

  florist foam

  florist tape

  small pinecones

  florist wire

  cinnamon sticks, cut to 2-inch lengths

  narrow silver or gold ribbon

  9 tall, dripless candles

  small spruce and/or fir branches

  holly and/or ivy sprigs

  1 dozen red roses

Select a bowl that is around 2 inches in diameter smaller than the plate and place in the center of the plate. Cut the florist foam into a circle and soak it in water for 5–10 minutes, then secure it to the bowl with a crisscross of floral tape.

Take the pinecones and bundle them into groups of three or four with florist wire, tying the stems together. Leave about 2

Beautifying Your Home

inches of wire coming off the end. Wrap the cinnamon sticks in groups of three with the ribbon.

Take 4 candles and cut 1½ inches off the bottom. Take 1 uncut candle and push it into the center of the foam. Arrange the 4 other uncut candles around it, making a circle. Then take the 4 shorter candles and push them into the foam near the edge, creating a square. From this point on, make sure that you look at the arrangement from all angles as you work so that the arrangement will be balanced.

Push the fir and/or spruce branches into the sides of the foam so that they are lying on top of the plate. Poke ivy and holly in the rest of the sides of the foam and around the candles to give body to the arrangement. Cut the stems of the roses so they are about 6 inches long. Push them into the foam among the candles and around the sides. Place the cinnamon sticks throughout to complete the centerpiece.

Holiday Napkin Rings

*T*hese will go beautifully with the centerpiece.

6 bendable tree twigs such as silver birch, long enough to have a 3-inch circumference when bent

floral wire

silver or gold ribbon

small dried red roses

glue gun

Twist twigs into rings and fasten with floral wire. Make a small bow with the ribbon and tie onto each of the rings. Make sure that when the ring is flat on the table, the bow is also horizontal. (If necessary, carefully hot-glue the bow.) Next, hot-glue a small bunch of dried roses around the bow and over the knot to create a splash of color. Makes 6 napkin rings.

> *Even if something is left undone, everyone must*
> *take time to sit still and watch the leaves turn.*
>
> —Elizabeth Lawrence

Rosemary Rings

For a holiday party, decorate your serving platters with rosemary rings. Simply shape long branches into a wreath and tie with floral wire. Place on plate and decorate branches with cherry tomatoes. Put food in center. You can also use shorter rosemary branches to make festive napkin rings; again secure with floral wire.

Beautifying Your Home

Easy Potpourri

Most potpourri have a major scent, often a secondary one and a fixative (usually orris root, available from most herb catalogs and stores). Roses, lavender, and orange blossoms are all common flowers for the major scents. The secondary scent is usually provided by something lighter—scented geranium, delphinium, lemon verbena, mint, and bay are common, but dry them before they fade.

You can use flowers from your garden or those from a bouquet. Spread on a rack, such as a cake rack, and let them dry in a warm but shady spot. This may take a week or longer—until the petals feel dry but have not turned brittle. You can continue to gather flowers until you have enough for all the potpourri you plan to make. Just store dried flowers in a sealed container in a dark place until ready to be used.

Mix the petals with the orris root and any other ingredients you want to add—bay leaves, cloves, allspice. For each quart of petals, use one tablespoon of orris root. Stir gently and store in an airtight container in a cool, dark place for about 3 weeks. Then place the potpourri in an attractive glass or ceramic jar that can be closed tightly. Open the jar to fill the room with fragrance; close it to preserve the potpourri. You can also package it up in a basket, with ribbons or raffia for gift giving.

Potpourri Supplies

Lavender Lane, PO Box 7265, Citrus Heights, CA 95621
($2 for catalog)

Rosemary House, 120 S. Market Steet, Mechanicsburg,
PA 17055 ($2 for catalog)

Indiana Botanic Gardens, PO Box 5, Hammond, IN
46325 (free)

Christmas Potpourri

1 quart dried pine needles

1½ teaspoons essential oil such as pine or fir

1 cup chopped patchouli leaves

½ cups cinnamon sticks, broken in halves

1 tablespoon each allspice, cinnamon, cloves, mace, and orris
root

handful of dried cranberries.

Combine the pine needles and oil in a large bowl, then add
rest of ingredients. Place in a potpourri jar or glass bowl.

Simmering Holiday Potpourri

Here's a mixture you can make for holiday gifts for teachers,
or for open houses and other get-togethers when you want to
bring a little something. Be sure to package with directions.

*Beautifying Your
Home*

1 cup whole allspice

1 cup star anise

1 cup ginger, cut into slices

2 cups orange peel, cut into slices

2 cups rose petals

2 cups lemon verbena leaves

30 drops allspice oil

Combine all ingredients except allspice oil in a large container. Stir in oil 5 drops at a time until mixture is well combined. Store in airtight container or, if you want to use as gifts, package in baggies or small jars.

To use, pour ⅔ cup into 2–3 cups of water and simmer gently on stove to release aroma. Can be reheated until scent is gone. Makes about 10 cups.

In a Japanese Garden

*I*n order to comprehend the beauty of a Japanese garden, it is necessary to understand—or at least to learn to understand—the beauty of stones. Not of stones quarried by the hand of man, but of stones shaped by nature only. Until you can feel, and keenly feel, that stones have character, that stones have tones and values, the whole artistic meaning of a Japanese garden cannot be revealed to you. At the approaches to temples, by the side of roads, before holy groves, and in all parks and pleasure-grounds, as well as in all cemeteries, you will notice large, irregular, flat slabs of natural rock—mostly from the river beds and water worn—sculptured with ideographs, but unhewn. These have been set up as votive tablets, as commemorative monuments, as tombstones, and are much more costly than the ordinary cut-stone columns and hakas chiseled with the figures of divinities in relief. Again, you will see before most of the shrines, and even in the grounds of nearly all large homesteads, great irregular blocks of granite or other hard rock, worn by the action of torrents and converted into water-basins (*chodzubachi*) by cutting a circular hollow in the top. Such are but common examples of the utilization of stones even in the poorest of villages; and if you have any natural artistic sentiment, you cannot fail to discover, sooner or later, how much more beautiful are these natural forms than any shapes from the hand of the stone cutter.

> *Join the whole creation of animate things in a deep, heartfelt joy that you are alive, that you see the sun, that you are in this glorious earth which nature has made so beautiful, and which is yours to enjoy.*
>
> —Sir William Osler

Beautifying Your Home

Zen Centerpiece

Truly nothing could be easier than this arrangement; it will foster serenity wherever you place it.

small dark rocks

colander

shallow bowl

3 small floating candles

1 flower such as a gardenia, rose, or hibiscus

Place the rocks in a colander and rinse. Take the bowl and fill the bottom with 1–2 inches of rocks, depending on the depth of the container—you want to create a rock bottom. Fill with water up to 1 inch from the top rim. Float the candles and gently place the blossom on the water and allow it to float.

Flowerpot Candles

Nothing can be easier than turning your old flowerpots into beautiful candle holders—wonderful for you and as holiday gifts. This is a Christmas holiday scent, but feel free to substitute your own favorite essential oils. This recipe is for one candle, but can be multiplied for more.

1 3-inch clay flowerpot

small piece of self-hardening clay

1 6-inch candle wick

1 small stick at least 5 inches long

1 ounce beeswax

1 ounce paraffin wax

15 drops cinnamon essential oil

15 drops mandarin orange essential oil

Plug the hole in the bottom of the pot with the clay and let harden. Attach one end of the wick to the stick. Lay the stick on top of the pot with the wick hanging down in the center of the pot.

In a double boiler, melt the beeswax and add paraffin. When melted, remove from heat and let cool slightly. Add the essential oils and mix thoroughly.

Pour the wax slowly into the pot, reserving a little bit. Fill to within ¼ inch of top. If a hollow forms around the wick as the wax cools, pour more wax into hollow. Once wax has hardened, remove stick by trimming the wick. Makes one candle.

Holiday Wreath

*T*his is your basic green wreath that can cost so much to buy. This year, why not try making one of your own?

wreath form

spooled green floral wire

evergreen boughs

Beautifying Your Home

garden trimming shears

wire cutters

decorations such as pine cones, holly, small ornaments, etc.

large bow

glue gun

Tie the end of the spool of floral wire around the wreath form. Pick up a small bunch of evergreen bough stems. Cut them about 3–5 inches in length and place them on the inside of the form. Wrap the wire around the form, over the boughs, a couple of times. Wrap tightly so the boughs are fairly secure. Gather another bunch of boughs, trim if necessary, and place next to the last bunch. Secure in place with wire. Repeat this, moving to the outside edge as you go. When you finish the first row, place the next bunch around 2 inches down from where you started and repeat the sequence again. Make sure that the stem ends and wire of the previous row is well covered. Continue until you have covered the whole wreath form. Tie off the wire and cut the excess off close to the knot.

Now you can decorate the wreath with trim of your choosing. With the glue gun, glue pine cones, holly, ornaments, etc., to the wreath. Glue on bow. When you are done, take the floral wire and pass a couple of loops of the wire around the wreath form to create a hanger. Check to be sure it can't be seen when you hang the wreath up.

Orange and Bay Garland

In the back woods of Maine, I've seen this Christmasy-smelling garland made into a wreath by shaping a wire clothes hanger into a circle and using it instead of twine. It requires a bit of advanced planning—you need to dry the oranges in a cooling oven after you've baked something else before assembling the rest.

3 oranges

metal skewers

1 yard string

8 cinnamon sticks

100 fresh bay leaves

1 large darning needle

Make a series of vertical cuts into the oranges but do not cut all the way through (Imagine sectioning an orange with the peel on, but go only ¼ of the way). Thread through one of the slits onto the skewers, and come out the back side through another

Beautifying Your Home

slit. Rest the skewers across a baking pan so that the oranges are suspended over the pan. Place in a cooling oven and let sit until the orange skins have hardened. Let sit in a warm, dry place for 1 week or so to continue drying.

To make the garland, tie a knotted loop at one end of the string. Tie a cinnamon stick on next to the loop. Thread the darning needle onto the other end of the string and then thread 10 bay leaves onto the string by skewering them through the middle with the needle. Tie another cinnamon stick on and thread another 10 bay leaves. Thread an orange through the center. Repeat until you've used up all the materials. Makes a 30-inch garland that can be tacked to a mantle.

Gardening gives me fun and health and knowledge. It gives me laughter and colour. It gives me pictures of almost incredible beauty.

—John F. Kenyon

Coaxing Spring

When you've got the winter blahs, say around February or March, one of the easiest cures is to anticipate spring by forcing branches to bring a bit of color indoors. Any of a wide variety of bushes, shrubs, and trees will do, including forsythia, crab apple, pussy willows, quince, cherry, plum, pear, dogwood, privet, red maple, gooseberry, weeping willow, and witch hazel. Simply cut the edges of the branches on a slant with sharp scissors and plunge immediately into a vase of warm water. As the days pass, make sure there is plenty of clean, tepid water in the vase and the warmth of the house will do the rest of the work. Voilà, instant spring!

> *How can one help shivering with delight when one's hot fingers close around the stem of a live flower, cool from the shade and stiff with newborn vigor!*
>
> —Colette

Beautifying Your Home

Nourishing Body and Soul

God has given us memories
that we may have roses in December.

—Anonymous

Grace in the Garden

I began gardening when I was forty, on my fortieth birthday to be exact. Up until then, gardening had always been something I did to have the yard look nice or to provide a place for the dogs to play. It was one of many hobbies I had, none of which were more central to my life than any other.

When I was thirty-nine, I went in for a routine physical as required by my employer. The intern found a tiny abnormality on my thyroid gland, which turned out to be malignant. I went through surgery to have the gland removed, then extensive recovery and testing. Soon after that it became apparent to me that I was going live for a while longer.

My fortieth birthday was approaching, and the only thing that seemed to make sense to me was to have my family and friends, those I so cherished in my life, plant a community vegetable garden with me on a long-unused portion of our yard. I

Nourshing Body
& Soul

was still physically weak, so would have to rely on the willingness and engagement of my community.

I have the fondest, most humbling, and powerful memories of that day and the days following. I remember my husband coordinating the whole day, making sure that the proper equipment, people, and food was available. I remember my mother and father cooking smoked mushrooms, a favorite of mine from New Orleans, so that I could have a special food on that day. I remember my brother-in-law, Randy, and my sister, Diane, coming very early, though they both had a very young son, so that Randy could help with rototilling and fertilizing ground that had not been worked in over ten years.

We planted rows of radishes, carrots, corn, cantaloupe, and squash, all from small plants. I can still see the herb garden going in as our friends from Redding, who had traveled over three hours to get there, designed and implemented an herb garden that was encircled with stone and love. And I remember the children, planting sunflower seeds that would grow over eight feet tall, children from the city who had never had the opportunity to find the magic of the soil.

I began my life again, there in that garden, just as the tiny plants and seeds began theirs. I spent at least an hour each evening in the garden, pulling weeds, or just talking to the plants. I could feel the love of my family and friends in each one of their pristine leaves. And the fruit of those plants was sweeter than any I could remember. That garden fed many, many families that year, and many, many hearts.

> *When bad things happen, it's the time when you*
> *get to work in the garden and sort out the pots*
> *from the weeds.*
>
> —Elizabeth Hurley

Aromatherapy Basics

Aromatherapy, the use of scents from the essential oils of plants to alter mood and promote healing, is an ancient art currently enjoying a booming revival. While many common garden plants are used in essential oils—peppermint, basil, and lavender, to name just a few—the quantities of flowers or leaves needed to produce the oil (1,000 pounds of jasmine flowers for one pound of oil, for example) means that even the most prolific gardeners would be better off buying their essential oils from catalogs or stores. Good sources include Bare Escentuals (800-227-3990); The Body Shop by Mail (800-541-2535); Casswell Massey Catalog (800-326-0500); Crabtree & Evelyn Catalog (800-272-2873); Frontier Cooperative Herbs: (800-786-1388); Green Mountain Herbs, Ltd. (800-525-2696); Hausmann's Pharmacy, Inc. (800-235-5522); SelfCare Catalog: (800-345-3371).

Nourshing Body
& Soul

Most commonly the oils are used in the bath (put in at the very end; the water should be no more than 100° F) or in a diffuser or placed on a handkerchief and inhaled when you need a lift. Since essential oils are very potent, they should always be diluted with a base oil such as sweet almond or grapeseed before being put on your skin. And don't ingest or get it in your eyes. If you are pregnant or have a chronic illness of any kind, consult your physician before using any.

Here are some of the most common essential oils and their qualities:

Basil: uplifting, clarifies thought processes

Bergamot: uplifting, yet calming

Cedarwood: relaxing, stress reducing

Camomile: soothing and calming, excellent to use after an argument

Eucalyptus: invigorating, cleansing, tonifying

Fennel: relaxing, warming, calming

Fir Needle: refreshing, cleansing

Frankincense: calming, releasing fear

Geranium: balancing mood swings, harmonizing

Juniper: purifying, stimulating

Lavender: calming, soothing, relaxing

Lemon: uplifting, refreshing, mental alertness

Lemongrass: stimulating, cleansing, tonifying

Lime: invigorating, refreshing

Mandarin orange: uplifting, refreshing

Marjoram: very relaxing, anxiety reducing

Myrrh: strengthening, inspiring

Orange: uplifting, refreshing

Patchouli: inspiring, sensuous

Pine: refreshing, cleansing, stimulating

Peppermint: stimulating, cleansing, refreshing, invigorating

Rose: emotionally soothing

Rosemary: stimulating, cleansing, good for studying, invigorating

Sage: cleansing, purifying

Sandalwood: Stress reducing, sensuous, soothing, helps release fear

Spearmint: refreshing, stimulating

Ylang-ylang: uplifting, sensuous

He wanted a flower garden of yellow daisies because they were the only flower which resembled the face of his wife and the sun of his love.

—Bessie Head

Nourshing Body & Soul

Kid-Safe Aromatherapy

With the popularity of aromatherapy these days, many parents are wondering if they are safe for children. Essential oils in particular can be quite strong and so there are a few guidelines:

1. Always dilute essential oils before applying to children's sensitive skin. You can use oils such as sweet almond, grapeseed, or jojoba for massage or skin care and liquid castile soap for shower products. But never put essential oils directly on a child's skin.

2. Shake well before using because the oils have a tendency to separate.

3. Keep all essential oils out of the reach of children. Ditto diffusers. Little children have been known to drink the oils in diffusers.

If you want to be sure the products you're using are safe for kids, try getting a catalog from Aromatherapy for Kids (800-955-8353) or Star Power Essentials (800-457-0904).

Juniper Bath Bag

Make the man in your life (or yourself) this extra-special treat this holiday season. It's amazingly simple—and if you have a bay tree, you can even get some of the ingredients from your own garden.

 ½ cup almond meal

10 drops patchouli oil

15 drops balsam oil

5 drops juniper oil

½ ounce shredded bay leaves

½ ounce juniper berries, crushed (use a mortar and pestle or the coffee grinder)

1 terry facecloth

½ yard string

Combine the almond meal and the essential oils in a glass bowl. Stir well with a wooden spoon to blend. Add the bay leaves and juniper berries and mix well. Open the facecloth and place on the counter. Pour the mixture onto the center of the cloth. Pick up the four corners and twist them closed as tightly as possible. Tie securely with string by winding it around several times and knotting firmly.

To use, fill up a tub with warm water until almost full. Add the bath bag, giving it a squeeze when wet. Rub the cloth over your body to remove rough skin. Delightful!

Nourishing Body & Soul

> *A happy life must be to a great extent a quiet life,*
> *for it is only in an atmosphere of quiet that true*
> *joy can live.*
>
> —Bertrand Russell

The Tao of Gardening

At one point in junior high, I became such an avid would-be gardener that I worked at a greenhouse during the summer and fancied becoming a landscaper. Working at the greenhouse was a real bonus as I got my pick of plants and trees that came in right off the truck. After they were deducted from my meager paycheck, I hardly made lunch money! I also got to adopt and rescue (for free!) plants that were becoming root-bound in the pot or whose health was becoming endangered by baking all day in too-sunny displays. I loved saving their lives and felt I was genuinely contributing to the health and beauty of the planet.

After a long summer of working, swimming, and gardening at home, I was glad to get back to the fall routine of school. I loved watching the season change toward the restful cold-weather time of winter. Aside from some mulching and pruning, there was nothing for me to do but sit back and watch the changes in my family's yard. My family was somewhat stunned by my gardening industry. With my supplies from the greenhouse, I had transformed an "okay" lawn into an impressive showplace, complete with a little Japanese multilevel Zen garden with a Japanese maple, a pond that didn't hold water very well, and the pièce de résistance—a chipped pagoda I'd gotten at the nursery!

When the winter snows hit, most of my efforts were hidden from view as my treasured plants took a well-deserved rest. After a two day blizzard, everything was under a white, fluffy blanket. My little Zen garden, however, still drew the eye. Finally, I understood the wisdom of Oriental gardeners. Their gardens were created to have changing beauty throughout all the seasons. I had only imitated what I had seen in the gardening books at the nursery. It was only in the dead of winter that I realized the red bark and leaves of the Japanese maple were stunningly beautiful against the blanket of snow. The pyracanthus climber I had planted was such a dark green as to almost be black with blazing orange berries while the evergreen shrubs, growing free form, took on an entirely eastern aspect next to the pagoda. Just looking at my little Zen garden in the snow filled me with inner peace.

Nature's Hangover Cure

Here's something to try, if necessary (hopefully not!), on New Year's Day.

1 tablespoon finely chopped fresh ginger root

1 teaspoon grated lemon peel

2 cups water

¼ cup culinary rose water

1 drop peppermint oil

Nourshing Body
& Soul

Combine the ginger root, lemon peel, and water in a covered pot and bring to a boil. Simmer 10 minutes. Strain out ginger and lemon peel pieces and cool the remaining liquid. Add rose water and oil of peppermint. Drink ½ cup at room temperature every 2 hours, along with plenty of water.

Restorative Bath

cotton bath bag

2 tablespoons grated fresh ginger

1 ounce fresh rosemary

20 drops rosemary oil

20 drops lavender oil

1 cup rose water

Place the fresh ginger and rosemary in a cotton bath bag, or bundle in a 1-foot-square piece of unused cheesecloth. Tie closed. Place the bag under the bathtub spigot and run under hot water. Add oils and rose water to the bath tub, swirling with your hand to combine. The bath bag makes an excellent scrubber and exfoliator, and the ginger and rosemary will leave skin pleasantly tingling and feeling revived.

Lessons from the Earth

*T*he season of reflection comes every year in northern California with the mid winter rain storms. When it is dark for days on end, and God seems to ask for contemplation, what has the year in my garden taught me?

I gaze out at the tiny peach tree that taught me this year to be more present with the earth. In the spring, I pruned the tree late and, when the rains stopped early, I neglected to pay attention: it almost died from lack of water. I spent all summer bringing it back from the dead, treating the tree with tender care, noticing when it needed water, picking off the little brown balls of sap that formed when an insect burrowed into a branch.

Soon it will be time to prune again, and this year I will notice which branches need to be trimmed. One or two should be plenty. Those left will be what is needed for the following year. Pruning is a lesson in moderation—you need to follow the need of the tree. Not too much, not too little.

I began the winter planting three kinds of beets. My parents occasionally had beets with a meal when I was a child. They were times I don't remember fondly—oh, how horrible the taste was. That round red slice would sit on my plate, and I would eat everything else so that I could say I was too full and how wonderful the meal had been. But my parents were onto my plan and that beet had to be consumed.

All these years later, my wife innocently made a meal with beets one day this year that she had bought at the farmers' market. What a revelation. Sweet, tender, with a flavor that seems to be all its own. How many years of beets I had missed because I

Nourshing Body & Soul

was convinced I didn't like them. What else has passed me by because my sense of self—I'm a person who doesn't like beets, I'm someone who always, who never—became too rigid? Now I grow beets of various colors to remind myself to stay open to life, to the ever-changing kaleidoscope of my being.

Lavender Lotion

Try buying some beautiful bottles with stoppers and decorate them with dried lavender sprigs and a raffia bow for a beautiful gift. This is so easy you can make it for everyone on your holiday list.

> 8 ounces unscented body lotion
>
> 30 drops lemon essential oil
>
> 30 drops lavender essential oil

Pour the lotion into a glass bowl and add the essential oils. Mix well. Using a funnel, fill container of choice, seal, and decorate. Makes 8 ounces.

Sleepy Time Potpourri

For help in sleeping, try this in a bowl in your bedroom. The lavender is said to dispel melancholy, the rosemary nightmares, and the chamomile and marjoram act as a soporific.

> 2 cups lavender flowers
>
> 2 cups rosemary (flowers and leaves)

1 cup chamomile flowers

2 tablespoons marjoram

2 teaspoons aniseed

2 teaspoons orris root

5 drops bergamot oil

Homemade Mint Lip-Balm

1 pound jar petroleum jelly

1 microwave-safe quart container

2 tablespoons dried mint

1 ounce shredded beeswax (available at craft stores)

piece of cheesecloth

1 quart container with spout

1 ounce aloe vera

20 drops liquid vitamin E

2 tablespoons witch hazel

tiny plastic containers with lids (available at hardware stores or craft stores)

Take the petroleum jelly out of its jar and place in a microwave-safe quart container. Set the microwave on 50% power and heat until the jelly is soft. Put the mint and the beeswax into the jelly and heat for one minute. Stir the jelly, then heat again for another minute. (Note: Stir with a non-metal spoon so as to not flavor the liquid.) Repeat until completely

Nourshing Body & Soul

melted. Take the cheesecloth and fold it in half. Strain the beeswax–petroleum jelly mixture through the cheesecloth into the quart container with spout. Discard cheesecloth. Stir in the remaining ingredients and pour into containers. Fills several containers, depending on size.

> *The roses under my window make no reference to former roses or better ones; they are what they are; they exist with God today. There is no time to them. There is simply the rose; it is perfect in every moment of its existence.*
>
> —Ralph Waldo Emerson

Visible Love

*I*t started out accidentally. In the first blush of romance, I sent my future wife a bouquet of long-stemmed roses. She couldn't bear to throw them out, so after a couple days, she took them out of the vase and dried them in a bunch from her kitchen rafters. The next time I sent her flowers, she did the same thing. Pretty soon it was a tradition—any time we gave one another flowers, she preserved them in bunches in the kitchen. Now, almost ten years later, every time I walk into the kitchen, I see a visible testment to our relationship—ten years of Valentine's Day roses; anniversary carnations; mixed bouquets to say welcome home, or I'm sorry, or no reason at all; and the sunflowers I gave her the day our daughter was born. Ten years of loving right in front of my eyes. Sometimes, in the midst of a fight, I go there just to be reminded, so I won't, in the heat of the moment, be tempted to throw it all away.

Valentine's Day Treats

Touch Me Massage Oil

>   4 ounces sweet almond oil
>
>   ½ teaspoon of your favorite essential oil

Blend well in a bowl and then pour into a small decorative glass bottle with a top. Add a beautiful ribbon, make a card, and present to the valentine of your choice. He or she will get the idea. Be sure to shake oil well before using.

Love Bath

>   1 cup dried lavender
>
>   1 cup dried rosemary
>
>   1 cup dried rose petals
>
>   ½ cup dried lovage
>
>   ½ cup dried lemon verbena
>
>   ¼ cup each dried thyme, mint, sage, and orris root
>
>   muslin

Nourshing Body & Soul

Mix all dried herbs together and store in a covered container. When you want to take a bath, place ¼ cup of herbal mix in the center of an 8-inch square of muslin and tie tightly with a piece of string. Boil this ball in 1 quart of water for 10 minutes. Draw a warm bath, pour in the herbal water, add you and your sweetheart, and use the ball to scrub one another's bodies. Makes 16 bath balls.

Valentine Love Bath

*H*ere's an aromatherapy bath to inspire sensuality and enhance sexual vitality. For added fun, take it together. Run a warm bath and when tub is nearly full, light some candles, turn off the lights, and add 15 drops cardamom oil, 10 drops ylang-ylang oil, and 10 drops patchouli oil. Relax into the water and surrender to the sensations.

Herbal-Bath Cold Remedy

  2 tablespoons dried eucalyptus

  4 tablespoons dried rosemary

  4 tablespoons dried lavender buds

  2 tablespoons dried rosebuds

Steep the above ingredients in boiling water for 30 minutes. Strain, and add the remaining liquid to a warm (not hot) bath.

Winter Solace

I live in New England, but winter has never been my favorite time of year. The view from my dining room window of all unrelieved gray and white really gets me down. So I decided to intentionally plan for winter when I re-did my side yard. There was already a tall pine as a backdrop (thank the powers that be for evergreens!) and against that I placed a hedge of winterberry. It's a kind of holly, and its shiny red berries remain on the bushes long after the leaves have fallen. It has the added benefit of attracting chickadees and juncos, my favorite winter birds. In one corner I planted a red jade crabapple, which has weeping branches that touch the ground. It's beautiful to look at even after the small, bright red fruit has finally fallen. And for the promise of spring, I put a weeping cherry in the center (I guess I'm a sucker for trailing branches!), which bursts into bloom when the weather finally gets warm.

Now, when the snow settles in, I sit at my dining-room table and look out at the scene of green, red, black, and white, and things just don't seem as bleak.

Other Shrubs for Winter Beauty

Wintersweet—actually flowers in the winter; prized for its sweet fragrance;

Westonbirt dogwood—has rich red stems that look beautiful against snow;

Nourishing Body & Soul

Hazel—has corkscrew branches that make a wonderful silhouette;

Cornus stolonifer—has bright yellow branches;

Sea buckthorn—lots of bright orange berries that last through the winter.

Honey-Sage Tea

This may not cure your cold or flu, but it sure will make you feel better:

2 tablespoons honey

juice of 1 lemon

1 ounce sage leaves, torn

boiling water

Place honey, lemon, and sage in a mug. Pour the water over and stir to dissolve honey. Cover and let sit for at least 5 minutes. Makes 1 mug of tea.

The Daydream Garden

I've always been a city dweller and an urbanite at heart, but I've had my dream country garden planned out in my head since I was a very little girl, down to the last stepping stone. It goes through different phases; sometimes it's a very structured and proper English garden, complete with boxed hedges and sweet, little meandering pebbled footpaths; other times I envision an austere yet serene Japanese garden, all twisted bonsai and reflective pools filled with ponderous carp. There are days when my garden is sunny and filled with flowers of all hues, and days when a gentle rain mists the knowing pines, ferns, and grasses. Changing my daydream garden is almost as fun as reflecting upon it; a year's worth of sunny annuals can be plucked up at a moment's notice and replaced by an elaborately terraced and exotic herb garden or row upon row of proud sunflowers. Best of all, it never needs watering, and the only pests are fat, lazy bumblebees. Someday I hope to have a real garden of my own, but I know that will never really rival the one in my head!

What I Get from a Garden

Visible gratitude.

Small surprises.

Metaphors.

Antidotes for too much thought.

A place to do some thinking.

A place to slash and burn and feel good about it.

Nourshing Body & Soul

A dozen shades of green.

Solvable problems.

More than I put in.

Permission to be muddy.

A model of God's efficiency and extravagance.

A chance to see the whole wheel turn.

A feast of color.

Encounters with interesting creatures.

Patience.

A place to "practice resurrection."

Zucchini for the whole neighborhood.

A place to practice strategy on small predators.

A chance to start over.

Acknowledgments

This book was truly a collaborative effort, which could not have grown and blossomed without Mark Akins, Suzanne Albertson, Ame Beanland, The Barnstable, MA. Grubs Garden Club, Jennifer Brontsema, Bill Edelstein, Julie Gleeson, Brenda Knight, Nina Lesowitz, Ann and Laura Marceau, Dawna Markova, Donald McIlraith, Marilyn Chandler McIntyre, Patricia Renton, Gloria and Vincent Ryan, and Barb Parmet, who provided me with original stories and suggestions. Many thanks.

Thanks also to Claudia Schaab, for able editorial assistance on this and all Conari book projects, and to my husband, who took pity on my hands and hunted and pecked much of the book for me.

Previously published contributions come from:

Mabel Osgood Wright in *The Garden of a Commuter's Wife.* © 1904. The Macmillan Co.

Ruth Stout in *Souvenirs: Gifts from the Garden* by Kathryn Kleinman & Michaele Thunen. © 1994 Kathryn Kleinman & Michaele Thunen. San Francisco: Collins Publishing.

Beverley Nichols in *Down the Garden Path*. NY: Doubleday. Copyright Beverley Nichols, 1932.

"Winter Garden", "Early Morning Garden", and "Clothes Line Lyric" by Barbara Bedayn. Copyright © 1996 by the family of Barbara Bedayn. Reprinted with permission of Rod Bedayn.

"A Seng Song Pot of Possibilities" from *POEMCRAZY* by Susan Wooldridge Copyright © 1996 by Susan G. Wooldridge. Reprinted with permission of Carol Southern Books, an imprint of Clarkson N. Potter, a division of Crown Publishers, Inc.

Thanks also to the talented Conari Press crew, both those already named as well as Heather Dever, Will Glennon, Annette Madden, Everton Lopez, Tom King, Jay Kahn, and Lara Morris.

INDEX

Resource Guide

Antique Rose Emporium (page 69)	800-441-0002
Aromatherapy for Kids (page 282)	800-955-8353
Bare Escentuals (page 279)	800-227-3990
Body Shop by Mail, The (page 279)	800-541-2535
Casswell-Massey Catalog (page 279)	800-326-0500
Casual Living (page 237)	800-843-1881
Cliff Finch Zoo (page 228)	209-822-2315
Cook's Garden, The (page 218)	802-824-3400
Cornell University, Laboratory of Ornithology (page 80)	607-254-2473
Crabtree & Evelyn Catalog (page 279)	800-272-2873
CSANA (Community Supported Agriculture) (page 15)	413-528-4374
Edmund Scientific Co. (page 222)˙	609-573-6250
Environmental Protection Agency (page 80)	800-490-9198
Frontier Cooperative Herbs (page 279)	800-786-1388
Garden Wheels (page 216)	800-723-8992
Gardener's Eden (page 237)	800-822-1214
Gardener's Supply Company (pages 218, 222, 237)	800-863-1700
Gardens for Growing People (page 23)	415-663-9433

GardensAlive! (page 218)   812-537-8650

Green Mountain Herbs (page 279)   800-525-2696

Harmony Farm Supply (page 218)   707-823-9125

Hausmann's Pharmacy, Inc. (page 279)   800-235-5522

Indiana Botanic Gardens (page 267)
   PO Box 5, Hammond, IN 46325

J.W. Jung Seed (page 34)   414-326-3121

Johnny's Selected Seed's (page 218)   207-437-4301

Lark (page 53)   800-284-3388

Lavendar Lane (page 267)
   PO Box 7265 Citrus Heights, CA 95621

Mountain Farms Inc. (page 237)   704-628-4709

National Audubon Society, Bird and Wildlife Information Center
   (page 81)   212-979-3080

National Home Gardening Club (page 236)
   12301 Whitewater Dr. Monnetonka, MN 55343

Native Seeds/SEARCH (page 38)   520-327-9123

Natural Garden Company, The (page 71)   707-766-9303

Orchids, Etc. (page 237)   800-525-7510

Park Seed (page 218)   800-845-3369

Peaceful Valley Farm Supply (page 218)   916-272-4769

Penzeys Ltd. (page 38)   414-574-0277

Plow & Hearth (page 78, 237)   800-627-1712

Prairie Moon Nursery (page 20)
   Rt. 2, Box 163, Winona, MN 55987

Real goods (page 222)   800-762-7325

Rosemary House (page 267)
   120 Market St. Mechanicsburg, PA 17055

Roayll River Roses (page 69)   800-820-5830

Seed Catalog, The (page 218)   800-274-7333

Seed Saver's Exchange (page 224)   319-382-5990

Seeds of Change (page 238)   888-762-7333

SelfCare Catalog (page 279)   800-345-3371

Shepard's Garden Seeds (page 218)   860-482-3638 (East Coast)
                                    408-335-6910 (West Coast)

Smith & Hawken (page 237)   800-776-3336

Spring Hill Nurseries (page 237)   800-582-8527

Sprouting for All Seasons (page 246)   801-295-9451

Star Power Essentials (page 282)   800-457-0904

Stonewall Chili Pepper (page 38)   800-232-2995

Sturdi-built Greenhouse (page 242)   800-722-4115

Sumway (page 34)   803-663-9771

Tomato Grower's Supply Company (page 218)   813-768-1119

Topiaries Unlimited (page 229)   802-823-5536

Topiary, Inc (page 229)
   41 Bering St., Tampa, FL 33606

Underwood Shade Gardens (page 20)   508-222-2164

Vermont Bean (page 34)   802-273-3400

White Flower Farm (page 218)   800-503-9624

Winterthur Museum & Gardens (page 237) 800-767-0500

Woodstock percussion (page 11) 800-422-4463

Conari Press, established in 1987, publishes books on topics ranging from spirituality and women's history to sexuality and personal growth. Our main goal is to publish quality books that will make a difference in people's lives—both how we feel about ourselves and how we relate to one another.

Our readers are our most important resource, and we value your input, suggestions, and ideas. We'd love to hear from you—after all, we are publishing books for you!

For a complete catalog or to be added to our mailing list, please contact us at:

CONARI PRESS
368 Congress Street, Fourth Floor
Boston, Massachusetts -02210

800-423-7087   Fax 877-337-3309
e-mail orders@redwheelweiser.com